Timeless
(Pen) Names

Also by Thomas Fensch ...

The Man Who Was Dr. Seuss:
The Life and Work of Theodor Geisel

The Man Who Was Walter Mitty: The Life and Work of James Thurber

The Man Who Changed His Skin: The Life and Work of John Howard Griffin

and ...

Steinbeck and Covici: The Story of a Friendship

Conversations with John Steinbeck

Essential Elements of Steinbeck

The FBI Files on John Steinbeck

Steinbeck's bitter fruit: from The Grapes of Wrath to Occupy Wall Street

Conversations with James Thurber

Of Sneetches and Whos and the Good Dr. Seuss: Essays on the Life and Work of Theodor Geisel

Behind Islands in the Stream: Hemingway, Cuba, the FBI and the crook factory

Oskar Schindler and His List: The Man, the Book, the Film, the Holocaust and Its Survivors

The Kennedy-Khrushchev Letters

War Diaries from Inside Hitler's Headquarters

... and others

Timeless (Pen) Names

The life and work of

Charles Lutwidge Dodgson,
Samuel Langhorne Clemens,
Eric Blair and Theodor Geisel

Thomas Fensch

New Century Books

Copyright 2018 by Thomas Fensch
All rights reserved. No part of this book may be reproduced or utilised in any form or by any means, electronic or mechanical, including photocopying or recording, or by any information storage and retrieval system, without written permission from the author and publisher.

ISBN: 978-0-9995496-8-1 (softcover)
ISBN: 978-0-9995496-9-8 (ebook)

New Century Books
8821 Rockdale Rd.
N Chesterfield, Va., 23236
newcentbks@gmail. com

Book design by Jill Ronsley, suneditwrite.com

"The Mystery of Lewis Carroll" by Jenny Woolf originally appeared in the free-use website *The Public Domain Review*.

Contents

Introduction		i
1	Charles Lutwidge Dodgson	1
	"Jabberwocky"	19
2	Samuel Langhorne Clemens	21
	"The Celebrated Jumping Frog of Calaveras County"	29
3	Eric Blair	39
	Orwell's Masterwork: *1984*	47
	Neologisms in *1984* ...	50
	Aftermath ...	52
	From *1984*	56
4	Theodor Geisel	58
Notes		99
Bibliography		103
Introduction Redux		107
About the author		109

Introduction

THEY WERE—AND STILL ARE—famous world-wide for their pseudonyms—their pen names:

- Two were from the United States, two from England;
- One was unmarried, one married but childless, one adopted a child, only one had a regular family;
- Two specialized in children's literature, two in adult literature;
- All traveled outside their home country;
- One died early, rushing to finish his masterwork while seriously ill;
- All spent years perfecting their craft;
- All developed their pen names in unique ways;
- One often refused to acknowledge his pen name—one used his pen name to hide his personal background, two others largely embraced their pseudonyms.

This, then, is the life, work and books of these four writers, each a genius, in his own way.

       —*Thomas Fensch*
       N. Chesterfield, Va.,
       November, 2017

(Their names are in a revised version of this Introduction, set behind the Bibliography.)

1

Charles Lutwidge Dodgson

CHARLES LUTWIDGE DODGSON ... James Playsted Wood wrote, in his biography, *The Snark Was a Boojum: A Life of Lewis Carroll* ...

... who was born in Daresbury, Cheshire, in the north of England, January, 27,1832, had only one head. Though he was to be two people, he had only two hands, two feet, and on most days the usual number of noses, fingers and toes.

If this sounds like nonsense, it should, for Charles Dodgson was also Lewis Carroll and Lewis Carroll means nonsense. He loved nonsense, created nonsense, talked nonsense when he had the right audience, and wrote the most delightful and sensible nonsense in the English language.

Charles Dodgson knew a man whose feet were so large he had to put on his trousers over his head. He knew that the Snark really was a Boojum, and he knew a queen who sometimes believed as many as six impossible things before breakfast. He knew the Jabberwock only too well, and he warned people solemnly to beware of the frumious Bandersnatch—which is as good a thing to beware of as anything else. Some of this may have been because Dodgson's birthday, so he said, came once every seven years, and always on the fifth Thursday in April.

Some of Dodgson's habits were peculiar. When he was very tired, he went to bed a minute after he got up. When he was even more tired than that, he went to bed a minute *before* he got up. Some of his tastes were unusual too. When he was hungry, he liked a bit of mustard with some beef spread thinly under it, though his favorite dish was salt with some soup spread over it. He loved small girls and detested small boys. He thought they were a mistake. He could not read too well which is awkward for a college professor, which he was. Once when a small girl sent him sacks and love and baskets of kisses, he thought she had written "a sack full of gloves and a basket full of kittens." And grew very confused.

Lewis Carroll was often as confused as Charles Dodgson was. He was apt to see things backwards or hear them inside out. He associated with clergymen and college teachers for he was one of each himself but also with artists, mad hatters, actresses, March hares, and chessmen and sometimes seemed unable to tell any of them apart. Mostly he knew a hawk from a handsaw but in some moods Charles Dodgson Lewis Carroll or Lewis Carroll Charles Dodgson, or Charles Lewis Dodgson Carroll—for he was a mathematician and doted on permutations and combinations—thought he could fly down High Street in Oxford on a handsaw and cut down dandelions with a hawk.

He knew Queen Victoria and her consort, Prince Albert, and once he had been the Duke of Wellington, who defeated Napoleon at Waterloo. At least he said he had been, so that is probably just as true as the story about the man who put on his trousers over his head. He also knew a small girl named Alice who followed a rabbit underground into one of the most famous adventures in history, and another Alice who walked right through a looking-glass into a world almost as strange as the one this side of the mirror.

Highlights of Dodgson's life

1832—January 27, born in Daresbury, Cheshire.

1943—Family moved to Croft, Yorkshire.

1844—Entered Richmond School.

1846—Entered Rugby.

1850—Matriculated at Christ Church, Oxford, January 24.

1852—Made student of Christ Church. First Class Honors in Mathematics, head of list, October.

1854—Received B.A. degree, December 18.

1856—Appointed mathematical lecturer Christ Church in March. Used Lewis Carroll for the first time in the magazine *The Train*. Ordered camera and photographic supplies March

17. Took first successful picture, June 3.

1857—Received M.A. degree.

1861—Ordained as Deacon in Church of England.

1862—Told story of Alice's adventures to Edith, Alice and Lorina Liddell on a river excursion up the Isis to Godstow, July 4. Began lettering and illustrating the manuscript copy of the story November 13.

1864—Gave manuscript copy of *Alice's Adventures Under Ground* to Alice Liddell, November 26.

1865—*Alice's Adventures in Wonderland* was published

1866—First printing of *Alice* in the United States.

1867—Toured on the continent and in Russia with Reverend Henry Liddell, July 12 to September 13.

1868—Father died in June. Sisters established family residence in Guildford, Surrey,

1869—*Phantasmagoria and Other Poems*, published.

1871—*Through the Looking-Glass and What Alice Found There,* published December 6.

1876—*The Hunting of the Snark* published in March.

1880—Abandoned photography.

1881—Resigned lectureship in Mathematics late November.

1882—Became Curator Christ Church Common Room.

1886—Facsimile edition of *Alice's Adventures Under Ground* published.

1887—*The Game of Logic* published.

1889—*Sylvie and Bruno* published.

1893—*Sylvie and Bruno Concluded* published.

1896—*Symbohc Logic, Part 1,* published.

1898—Dodgson died July 14, in Guilford.

2015 was the 150th year anniversary of the first publication of *Alice's Adventures in Wonderland.* That same year, the website *The Public Domain Review* featured the essay "The Mystery of Lewis Carroll," by Jenny Woolf. Her charming and insightful essay is worth reprinting in full:

The Mystery of Lewis Carroll

When Charles L. Dodgson was born in January, 1832, his paternal aunt wrote a letter to his parents, welcoming the "dear little stranger" and begging them to kiss him on her behalf. His clergyman father, already "overdone with delight" whenever he looked at his family, put a notice in *The Times* to announce the arrival of his much-wanted first son.

The baby would grow up to become Lewis Carroll, author of two of the most famous children's books in the world. Mystery and even controversy, would surround him in later life, but one thing that never changed was his deep attachment to the members of his family, or theirs to him.

For his first eleven years, the Dodgsons lived in a small parsonage in the midst of fields, in the scattered village of Daresbury, Cheshire. The parsonage burned down over a hundred years ago, but its site still remains, marked out in bricks and enclosed in a decorative iron fence, with countryside all around.

Its rooms are tiny, for Charles' father was only a poor curate, and he had to take in pupils and grown some of his own food. But Charles remembered Daresbury Parsonage as a happy spot an "island farm, 'midst seas of corn." He and an ever growing number of brothers and sisters roamed the surrounding countryside, and his sisters remembered him as a typical boy, climbing trees and playing in local ponds. After his father was promoted, the family moved to a large rectory in the village of Croft-on-Tees, in Yorkshire, and soon grew to eleven children.

Charles was very young when he seems to have decided to become the family's main entertainer. He amused is brothers and sisters tirelessly, creating elaborate games for them to play in the garden telling them stories and creating magazines for them. His own youthful contributions to these magazines occasionally show hints of what was to come. Alice's Duchess, who saw a "moral" in everything, echoes his poem "My Fairy," written at the age of thirteen, in which he gently criticizes the explicit moralizing of contemporary children's books.

I have a fairy by my side
Which says I must not sleep.
When once in pain I loudly cried
It said, "You must not weep."

... When once a meal I wished to taste
It said, "You must not bite."
When to the wars I went in haste
It said, "You must not fight."

"What may I do?" at length I cried,
Tired of the painful task.
The fairy quietly replied
And said "You must not ask."

Moral: "You mustn't."

From all accounts, Charles relished the role of older brother, and his siblings are reported to having thought a lot of him; they certainly stayed close touch all his life. It seems that he was markedly protective, for as a schoolboy he was known for getting into fights in defense of smaller boys. Later in life, friends sometimes commented on how well he looked after them—one niece affectionately compared him to a "mother hen".

He had much in common with some of his sisters, and was less keen on the countryside sports his brothers liked. An early anti-vivisectionist, he shared a concern for animal welfare with his youngest sister Henrietta.

Schooling was not compulsory at the time, but it was better for a boy to attend school if he wanted to have a professional career. Charles was mostly educated at home, but when he was twelve he was sent to a little school in nearby Richmond, where he boarded with the headmaster, his wife and family, and was very happy.

By contrast, he loathed the three years he spent at boarding-school in Rugby. He did well, and won prizes, but he hated the school's lack of privacy, uninspired teaching, and savage bullying. Years later, he admitted it had not been totally bad, for he had made some friends, but he added that "no earthly considerations" would ever induce him to repeat the years he had endured there.

At nineteen, he went up to Christ Church, Oxford, his father's old college. He did very well, and before long was appointed a Fellow, known as a "Student", and was engaged in teaching mathematics. As he moved further into his twenties and got more involved in the job, he remained close to his family making the long trip back North during vacations, and socializing with his bothers and sisters at other times.

It is hard to know what he realty thought about Christ Church. It did offer opportunities to read, reflect and use his mind, and, in making a success of his life there, he was doing what he and his family expected. It also offered him the chance to meet many of the well known figures of the time, and his circle of friends does include large numbers of famous people. And he needed a decent salary, for his father had little money, and, as the oldest son, he knew he would assume responsibility for everyone after his father died.

On the other hand, the college was almost all-male and child-free, and may have seemed emotionally rather bleak. In order to comply with the college's archaic rules, he most reluctantly took Holy Orders, and knew he would be obliged to remain unmarried and celibate as long as he stayed in the job.

Teaching the undergraduates did not suit him, for with his quiet voice, gentle manner and troublesome stammer, he found it hard to keep order. Some of his rougher contemporaries made fun of his speech difficulty, and many of the undergraduates were rich young men who did not want to learn and considered themselves better than him. He seems to have coped with the emotional discomforts of his life by presenting a cold, remote face to those he did not know well.

He wrote his brothers and sisters long, entertaining letters, got involved in college politics and spent as much time as possible with the Liddell children. Harry, Ina, Edith and Alice, who lived in the college Deanery. With them, he could be more like his real self, the person he showed to his family. He took the children out, helped with all kinds of projects, and made up stories for them.

So this was the outward appearance of the man who created the story of "Alice in Wonderland" in 1862, when he was thirty years old. The famous story is said to have been told during a boating trip on July 4, when Charles, his friend Duckworth and the three Liddell girls rowed to the village of Godstow. Actually the story may have taken shape over two trips that summer—but in any case, the children loved it.

Alice Liddell was ten at the time, three years older than the "Alice" of the story. She was a clever, artistic little girl, with short dark hair, and bold confident gaze. And Charles was very found of her. When she pestered him to write the story out for her he did, although it was over two years before he arrived at the Deanery with his pretty handwritten volume of *Alice's Adventures Under Ground*.

It has sometimes been suggested that Charles was in love with Alice, or wanted to marry her as she grew older, but there is no evidence for this at all. In fact, he may only have named the character "Alice" to please his little friend, for he later took pains to point out that Alice the child was not the Alice he imagined in the story. His own contemporary illustrations, too, show Alice with long fairish hair, quite unlike Alice Liddell's dark bob.

He stayed friends with Alice's older sister Lorina for the rest of his life, and in fact gossip did circulate that he might have had his eye on her. It was unusual for a man in his position to seek out children's company so publicly, and many people thought he must have hopes of either the oldest girl or the governess. No evidence exists to back this up, but it is known that the friendship with Alice withered as she left childhood behind. He was not an important part of her family's social circle, and there are hints that she did not particularly like being world-famous because of someone else's book.

Charles did not record Alice's reaction to his gift, but many other people who saw the story loved it; so many, indeed, that he had already decided that he would publish it by the time he'd presented it to Alice. The publisher Alexander Macmillan agreed to work on it, although the agreement was that Charles would have to pay most of the cost of production.

Charles boldly committed over a year's salary to the project. Then, he scrapped the whole first edition of 2000, because Tenniel disliked the quality of the printing. Fussiness was one of his personal characteristics, as were a certain impetuousness, boldness, and a determination to do what he felt was right however inconvenient and difficult it might be.

When the book first appeared, Charles was not optimistic about its prospects. He thought he would lose about 200 (pounds), which was a huge sum then. He might recoup the loss if sales were exceptionally good, "but that," he concluded grimly, "I can hardly hope for."

Famous last words! Eventually Alice enabled him to retire early, although it didn't make a fraction of the money a bestseller would generate today. Within a decade, Charles' pseudonym of "Lewis Carroll" was a household name and when he died in 1898, the book and its sequel *Through the Looking Glass were* world-famous. They are now available all over the world, both in the original unaltered mid-Victorian texts and in numerous rewritings, and adaptions, movies, artworks, musicals, and animations.

As the books' fame grew, people naturally wondered about the man who had written them but Charles had no intention of revealing himself to the public. Writing a children's book did not particularly enhance his professional career and he flatly refused to acknowledge in public that he was "Lewis Carroll."

In fact, as far as his daily life went, "Lewis Carroll" was a complete non-person. Charles was always known personally only by his real name, letters directed to the pseudonym were returned unanswered, and he would walk away if strangers dared to mention "Alice" in his presence.

As the years went on, interest in him did not lessen and he presented an even more off-putting, grave, moralistic image to the outside world, and indeed, to many of his colleagues at Christ Church.

It has sometimes been wondered why he went to these lengths. Part of the reason seems to have been a need for privacy. After all, he lived in a semi-communal setting, and often spent time with his large extended family, as well. He dreaded being accosted by strangers, and he treasured periods of solitude in order to work on the mathematics which fascinated him.

He also wanted freedom from outside scrutiny. Within the circle of family, children and his many bohemian and artistic friends, he was teasing, humorous, sometimes emotional, occasionally reckless and iconoclastic. These were not qualities expected of staid, clerical academics in the restrictive world of the Victorian middle class. In this way, perhaps the sentiments of "My Fairy" applied to him, even in adult life.

In particular, his love of the theater and his passion for theatrical people created a problem so far as his public image was concerned. Theaters were not respectable in the mid-nineteenth century, and the plays they presented were often trivial and frivolous. Even though their reputation improved during his lifetime, his parents and most of his sisters never attended one in their lives.

But for him, the theater was a whole fantasy world. And the actors were its inhabitants. He was a perceptive, knowledgeable critic of their work, and he was also a most gifted and dramatic storyteller himself. In different circumstances, he might have been professionally involved with the stage, but this was impossible in the life he actually had.

The few adults to whom he told stories remembered him as a remarkable raconteur with a funny story for every occasion and the ability to render a listener to helpless laughter. He could also gather an audience with great ease, when he chose, as Ruth, daughter-in-law of the Victorian architect Alfred Waterhouse, described in a memoir.

As a little girl, she once arrived at a children's party and saw a pale old clergyman in black clothes. She glumly assumed he would spoil everything. Yet, "the party soon became Mr. Dodgson's party," she said, "and he talked so fascinatingly, that "I remember how exasperating it was to be asked whether I would like another piece of cake, when I was trying so hard to hear what he was saying."

Although he had several child friends who were boys, he made no secret of the fact that he preferred female company, and his nephew biographer also took the unusual step (for the time) of pointing out most of his friends were ladies.

He relaxed in the presence of females across all ages, and his bachelor rooms at Christ Church contained hundreds of books of poetry, myth, magic and legend, and toys and fancy dresses. At a time when the line between the sexes was firmly drawn, he had no interest in sport and war, but enjoyed fairies, animals, dressing up, art and beauty as well as puppets, dolls and stuffed toys. Even when he was an old man, his niece Irene remembered what fun it was crawling with him on the floor, playing with a toy bear. And it is perhaps significant that the only toy from his childhood that he bothered to photograph was a boy doll or puppet called "Tim."

As well as his passion for the theater, he was also a keen photographer mostly of people and particularly of children. Some of his young models remember how successfully he kept them interested and occupied during what was then a long and boring process, and parents sometimes commissioned him professionally to photograph their children. His nude images of children seem controversial today but nudes of both sexes and all ages were acceptable as valid subjects then, and in fact, some of the child images of his respectable contemporary Julia Margaret Cameron seem far more startling to the modern eye.

However, his love of children and his admiration for child nudity are sometimes taken to be evidence that he was a paedophile. It is impossible for anyone to know the definite truth about the sexual life of another particularly someone long dead and from a different culture. But again and again, children who knew him, including those photographed nude by him, remember him with real love and affection, in recollections that indicate he did not in any way behave like a paedophile. As Evelyn Hatch, who he photographed nude as "Odalisque" recalls, "what I remember most about Mr. Dodgson was his kindness ... his aim was to give happiness and to make life richer ... he was an ever-welcome guest." Dozens of other recollections of little girls echo this.

In general, he seems to have had a positive, constructive attitude, and he made the best of his life. But in some essential ways, he could not be himself, and his family said that he suffered periodically from black depression. At these times, they felt that the sincere love this child friends kept him going.

His affection, in turn, meant a great deal to many of them. Time and again they report that he took them seriously when nobody else did, and understood their points of view. Among many touching memories are those of Ethel, niece of Mathew Arnold, who recalls how "the hours spent in his dear and much-loved company, (were) oases of brightness in a somewhat grey and melancholy childhood."

He never married, and apparently never wanted to. Victorian marriage (with the prospect of many more dependents) would certainly have been a heavy addition to the constraints under which he already lived. It would have lost him what independence he had, and the mere fact of being married at all would have presented him with serious practical problems for many years. His closeness to his siblings might also have been a contributing factor to the decision. Only three of the eleven ever wed and the remaining seven remained under his care for the rest of his life.

However, as he grew older, he acquired many lady friends. This sometimes led to mild controversy. Victorian social life was highly formal, and it was thought improper for eligible men to have unchaperoned adult female friends.

During his youth he had been unable to spend time alone with respectable women, but after he passed what Victorians considered to be the age of "romance," he openly went on holiday with women friends, and gathered a sizeable circle of admiring ladies around him. As author Laurence Hutton recalled in 1903, shortly after his death "he liked young women, who all liked him, and Oxford is now full of women, mature and immature, who adore the gentle memory of the creator of 'Alice.'"

In later life, although he was kind, generous and involved to those close to him, he became increasingly difficult, eccentric and annoying to outsiders. He also began spending considerable time fretting about tiny moral points and examining finer points of his own conscious As he saw his own death approaching, he became very anxious not to offend God in any way. Much of his later fiction—self-conscious, badly structured, and over-moralistic—reveals this anxiety.

It was a relief to him to escape into the intellectual study of logic, which increasingly gripped him. But he still relaxed and seems to have gained strength from the company of the children he loved, and he continued to tell them original, funny, startling, and brilliant tales to make them happy. Adults rarely heard them, but his close friend Gertrude Thomson described them as being "like rainbows"—unique, beautiful, and evanescent.

He never wrote any of these tales down, and in a rare burst of confidence not long before he died he told Gertrude Thomson that he didn't know what people saw in the "Alice" books. Yet although he apparently chose to regard them as unimportant fairy tales, we know that *Alice's Adventures in Wonderland* and its companion *Through the Looking Glass* were both created at times of great personal stress for him. It is reasonable to assume that they were in some way therapeutic, and perhaps he did not want to think too deeply about what they represented.

Although he never wanted to discuss them with adults, he always wanted them to reach the widest possible child audience. And over the last 150 years, millions have grown up on "Alice". Many of these have gone on to produce their own works of art inspired by the curious little girl. To many of us, the wonderful variety of these cultural works makes a fascinating study—one that is nearly, though not quite, as interesting as the study of Dodgson himself.

Controversy about his fascination—or obsession—with little girls began during his lifetime and continues to this day. (He thought little boys were vile creatures.) There is no evidence whatsoever that he ever abused or mistreated them in any way. If he had not had this fascination—or obsession—with the real Alice and her friends and other little girls he met over the years, the world may never have had the two Alice books, to enjoy over the past 150-plus years and will have to enjoy far into the future.

And what of his pen name—his pseudonym—Lewis Carroll? How did he conjure it up?

He translated Charles Lutwidge into Latin, which became Carolus Ludovicus, and then "re-translated" them again as Carroll Lewis—and then reversed the names to Lewis Carroll, a small exercise in Dodgson's imagination.

"Jabberwocky"

It is perhaps the most famous nonsense poem ever written, and appeared in *Through the Looking Glass*. Few—if anyone at all—understand the true meaning. Perhaps Dodgson himself didn't know exactly what it meant. And many, many others may not know how to pronounce the words Dodgson made up for this poem. At best, perhaps, it's a fight between a knight, and a dragon, or other monster.

He did use—invent—one word which is now part of our common language: *chortle*, meaning *to chuckle gleefully*.

> 'Twas brillig, and the slithy toves
> Did gyre and gimble in the wabe:
> All mimsy were the borogoves,
> And the mome raths outgrabe.
>
> "Beware the Jabberwock, my son!
> The jaws that bite, the claws that catch!
> Beware the Jubjub bird, and shun
> The frumious Bandersnatch!"
>
> He took his vorpal sword in hand;
> Long time the manxome foe he sought—
> So rested he by the Tumtum tree
> And stood awhile in thought.

And, as in uffish thought he stood,
The Jabberwock, with eyes of flame,
Came whiffing through the tulgey wood,
And burbled as it came!

One, two! One, two! And through and through
The vorpal blade went snicker-snack!
He left it dead, and with its head
He went galumping back.

"And hast thou slain the Jabberwock?
Come to my arms, my beamish boy!
O frabjous day! Callooh! Callay!"
He chortled in his joy.

'Twas brillig, and the slithy toves
Did gyre and gimble in the wabe:
All mimsy were the borogoves,
And the mome raths outgrabe.

2

Samuel Langhorne Clemens

MARK TWAIN, William Faulkner once said, was "the first truly American writer, and all of us since are his heirs." Ernest Hemingway said much the same: "All modern literature comes from one hook by Mark Twain called *Huckleberry Finn*. All American writing comes from that. There was nothing before. There has been nothing as good since."

Twain, (Samuel Langhorne Clemens, Nov. 30, 1835–April 21, 1910), was born just three years after Charles Lutwidge Dodgson, in the tiny village of Florida, Missouri. He grew up in Hannibal, on the Mississippi, which later became the fictionalized locale of his novels *The Adventures of Tom Sawyer* (1876) and *The Adventures of Huckleberry Firm* (1885).

At 12, Twain left school (after the fifth grade) to become a printer's apprentice. (At that time, type was set letter-by-letter and had to be set upside down. The phrase "mind your p's and q's" was a warning to young apprentices who could be easily confused by the metal sticks of type. The phrase might well have been "mind your b's and d's"; the logic and warning was the same). Beyond setting type, he began contributing articles and sketches to *The Hannibal Journal*, which was owned by his brother Orion.

He then became something of an itinerant printer setting type in various cities, including New York, Philadelphia, St. Louis and Cincinnati and educating himself in various public libraries, in various cities where he stayed temporarily.

Back in Missouri, Twain had only one ambition; to be a riverboat pilot. Riverboat pilot Horace Bixby took Twain on as an aspiring pilot for $500, to be taken out of Twain's first earnings. Twain learned all the bends, depths, shoals, twists and turns of the Mississippi from St. Louis to New Orleans, and in the process found his pen name. "Mark Twain" was a common boatman's term; the cry that the water's depth was 12 feet or two fathoms, a safe level for steamboats. It took him more than two years to earn his pilot's license.

He convinced his brother Henry to also become a riverboat man. But Twain's brother was killed in June, 1858 when the boilers in the steamboat Pennsylvania exploded. Twain believed it was his fault for convincing his brother to join him on the Mississippi; it is said he carried the guilt for his brother's death throughout the rest of his life.

(It was only the first of a chain of family tragedies in Twain's life. He met Olivia "Livy" Landon Dec. 31, 1867. They were married in 1870; later the same year their first child, a son, Langdon was born. In 1872, their first daughter Susy was born, but Langdon died of diphtheria the same year. In 1874, a daughter Clara was born; in 1880, daughter Jean was born. In, 1896, Susy died of meningitis while Twain was lecturing in Europe. It is said he never fully recovered from her loss. In 1904, Livy died after a two-year illness. In 1906, daughter Jean was institutionalized due to severe epilepsy; she died in a bathtub in 1909 during a seizure. Only one daughter, Clara, survived Twain's death. His wife and all the other children died during his lifetime.)

His Mississippi boatman's career ended with the advent of the Civil War, but it gave him material for his later book *Life on the Mississippi* (1883).

He then joined his brother Orion in Nevada; Orion had become Secretary to Nevada Territorial Governor James W. Nye. Twain's trek ended in Virginia City Nevada, where he worked as a miner on the Comstock Lode and wrote for the Virginia City newspaper, *The Territorial Enterprise*. He first used the pseudonym Mark Twain there.

His experiences on the Mississippi led to *Life on the Mississippi*; his adventures in the west led to *Roughing It*, published in 1872. In Angels Camp in Calaveras County, California, he heard a tale that become one of his most famous short stores, "The Celebrated Jumping Frog of Calaveras County," which was published in the New York City weekly *The Saturday Press* November 18, 1865 and earned him international fame.

Twain then traveled to the Sandwich Islands, now present-day Hawaii, and contributed a series of articles to *The Sacramento* (California) *Union* newspaper.

Returning to California, he began a series of lectures, which he continued throughout his life.

In *Mark Twain's San Francisco*, (McGraw-Hill, 1963) Bernard Taper writes:

> It was as Samuel Clemens that he had stepped off the stagecoach in Nevada. It was as Mark Twain that he came on to San Francisco That name—probably the most famous pen name in the history of literature

and one that feels to us now as the most apt somehow, the most "right"—he had adopted in Virginia City just the year before, because pseudonyms were the thing among the local columnists (it first appeared in print February 2, 1893). The pseudonym still sat new on him; he had not really broken it in yet. By the time he left San Francisco a few years later he wore the name most naturally; it had become one that fitted not only the writing that developed here but his personality as well.

Taper also writes:

> Parody, burlesque, fantasy, the tall tale—these forms, which Twain was to employ all his life, even in his more serious works, are prominent in his San Francisco writings; his increasing deftness in their use may be noted. In many respects, these early pieces of journalism, intended as fugitive and casual reports, stand up as well or better than the later essays he polished and worked over. They are directly engaged in a way that many of the later writings are not: they had *real* topics. They are less inflated than some of the later essays and there is less striving to be oracular.

Twain fell in love with Livy Langdon when he first saw a photograph of her. Back in the east, they corresponded during 1868; she rejected his first marriage proposal but they were married, in 1870. She was from a wealthy liberal family.

They moved to Hartford, Connecticut in 1873, where Twain began building a home; They spent the summers in Elmira, New York, in the home of Livy's sister, Susan Crane.

The years—1874–1891, in Hartford—were perhaps Twain's most productive. He wrote: *The Adventures of Tom Sawyer*, 1876; *The Prince and the Pauper*, 1881; *Life on the Mississippi*, 1883; *The Adventures of Huckleberry Finn*, 1885; and *A Connecticut Yankee in King Arthur's Court*, 1889, all during that period.

Huckleberry Finn, published in 1885, is now considered one of the greatest novels in American literature, yet not without its critics. Twain began it in 1876, but put it away for several years before completing it.

To this day, *Huckleberry Finn* has been banned and banned again and again from schools and libraries, largely because of *that word: nigger*, common enough in Twain's time, especially during and after the Civil War, but obviously unacceptable today. Joseph Conrad's novel, *The Nigger of the "Narcissus,"* first published in 1897, has met the same fate, clearly for the title alone.

Clemens must have thought *Huckleberry Finn* was almost an impossible project; he first thought it to be a sequel to *Tom Sawyer*, but it wasn't quite a sequel. He began the project, then abandoned it for several years. He first thought to continue Huckleberry Finn into adulthood, then abandoned that. He worked on *Huckleberry Finn* off and on from 1876 to 1884.

As Justin Kaplan writes in *Mr. Clemens and Mark Twain*:

> I am tearing along on a new book (Twain) told Mary Fairbanks on August 4 (1876) about his second

project of the summer. He could not afford any interruptions he said, because he was afraid his mill might get cold. Five days alter he was writing to (William Dean) Howells in a more casual spirit.

Began another boy's book—more to be at work than anything else. I have written 400 pages on it—therefore it is very nearly half done. It is Huck Finn's Autobiography. I like it only tolerably well as far as I have got, and may possibly pigeonhole or burn the MS when it is done." The tank ran dry, as he feared and though he did not burn the manuscript he did pigeonhole it for two years; he worked on it again in 1879 or 1880, pigeonholed it again, and finally finished it in 1884, eight years and seven books after he first began it, a wandering process of creation that is a book-length story in itself. In the first sixteen or so chapters that Clemens wrote that first summer and liked "only tolerably well," he set Huck Finn and Jim afloat on their raft, their fragile island of freedom between the two shores of society, When they passed Cairo, Illinois, in the night, the last free-soil outpost, Mark Twain found himself faced with an enormously difficult problem of plot and structure. He solved that problem with a persistence which reveals his deep involvement with the book both as a literary artist and as a man desperately needing to resolve his own bewilderments about conscience and the restraints and freedoms of the community.

He eventually intended it to focus on racism, bigotry, slavery, and the post-Civil War years, by then gone; all told in *patois* by a semi-literate boy—Huckleberry Finn. To have the narrator a uneducated boy was unique to American literature.

In *Was Huck Black?* Shelly Fisher Fishkin writes:

> Although commentators differ on the question of which models and sources proved most significant, they tend to concur on the question of how *Huckleberry Finn* transformed American literature. Twain's innovation of having a vernacular-speaking child tell his own story *in his own words* was the first stroke of brilliance; Twain's awareness of the power of satire in the service of social criticism was the second. Huck's voice combined with Twain's satiric genius changed the shape of fiction in America.

And, she writes:

> Mark Twain helped open American literature to the multicultural polyphony that is its birthright and special strength. He appreciated the creative vitality of African-American voices and exploited their potential in his art. In the process, he helped teach his countrymen new lessons about the lyrical and exuberant energy of vernacular speech, as well as about the potential of satire and irony in the service of truth. Both of these lessons would ultimately

make the culture more responsive to the voices of African-American writers in the twentieth century. They would also change its definitions of what "art" ought to look and sound like to be freshly, wholly "American."

Twain lectured throughout much of his life, earning substantial sums from his books and lectures; driven to lecture to pay expenses. Much of his earnings had to be used to stave off losses from imprudent investments; He invested heavily—$300,000—which would be about $8,000,000 in today's money—in the Paige Compositor, a mechanical typesetting machine, which was complex and was prone to malfunctions and breakdowns. It was a forerunner to the Linotype machine, a much more efficient and reliable machine. Twain also invested in the Charles Webster publishing company, which he established. It too, failed after ten years. Henry Huttleston Rogers helped get him out of bankruptcy; Twain paid off all his pre-bankruptcy creditors. Legally he had no obligations to do so, but morally felt it necessary.

After *Huckleberry Finn*, Clemens, as Mark Twain, published: *A Connecticut Yankee in King Arthur's Court* (1889); *Pudd'nhead Wilson* and *Tom Sawyer Abroad*, (1894); *Personal Recollections of Joan of Arc* (1896); *Following the Equator* (1897); and *Eve's Diary* (1906).

Samuel Clemens—forever Mark Twain—died April 21, 1910, at 74.

Huckleberry Finn has become his masterwork—and permanently changed American literature. But during his lifetime—and today—it continues to be one of the most banned books extant; banned in libraries and public schools, largely because of his use of one word: *nigger*.

"The Celebrated Jumping Frog of Calaveras County"

When Samuel Clemens was working as a miner in Angels Camp, California, he heard a tale about a jumping frog. He reworked it as "The Celebrated Jumping Frog of Calaveras County"; it was published in New York in *The Saturday Press*, in 1865. It was his first nationally-published short story and brought him national—and international—fame. It was published throughout the United States and subsequently published in England and translated into French.

All writers love to tinker, revise and edit their work; this is an 1865 version, first titled "Jim Smiley and His Jumping Frog."

Mr. A. Ward,

Dear Sir:—Well, I called on good-natured, garrulous old Simon Wheeler, and inquired after your friend, Leonidas W. Smiley, as you requested me to do, and I hereunto append the result. If you can get any information out of it you are cordially welcome to it. I have a lurking suspicion that your Leonidas W. Smiley is a myth—that you never knew such a personage, and that you only conjectured that if I asked old Wheeler about him it would remind him of his infamous Jim Smiley, and he would go to work and bore me nearly to death with some infernal reminiscence of him as long and tedious as it should be useless to me. If that was your design, Mr. Ward, it will gratify you to know that it succeeded.

I found Simon Wheeler dozing comfortably by the bar-room stove of the old, dilapidated tavern in the ancient mining camp of Boomerang, and I noticed that he was fat and bald-headed, and had an expression of winning gentleness and simplicity upon his tranquil countenance. He roused up and gave me good-day. I told him a friend of mine had commissioned me to make some inquiries about a cherished companion of his boyhood named Leonidas W. Smiley—Rev. Leonidas W. Smiley—a young minister of the Gospel, who he had heard was at one time a resident of this village of Boomerang. I added that if Mr. Wheeler could tell me any thing about this Rev. Leonidas W. Smiley, I would feel under many obligations to him.

Simon Wheeler backed me into a corner and blockaded me there with his chair—and then sat me down and reeled off the monotonous narrative which follows this paragraph. He never smiled, he never frowned, he never changed his voice from the gentle-flowing key to which he tuned the initial sentence, he never betrayed the slightest suspicion of enthusiasm—but all through the interminable narrative there ran a vein of impressive earnestness and sincerity, which showed me plainly that, so far from his imagining that there was any thing ridiculous or funny about his story, he regarded it as a really important matter, and admired its two heroes as men of transcendent genius in finesse. To me, the spectacle of a man drifting serenely along through such a queer yarn without ever smiling was exquisitely absurd. As I said before, I asked him to tell me what he knew of Rev. Leonidas W. Smiley, and he replied as follows. I let him go on in his own way, and never interrupted him once:

There was a feller here once by the name of Jim Smiley, in the winter of '49—or maybe it was the spring of '50—I don't recollect exactly, somehow, though what makes me think it was one or the other is because I remember the big flume wasn't finished when he first came to the camp; but any way, he was the curiousest man about always betting on any thing that turned up you ever see, if he could get any body to bet on the other side, and if he couldn't he'd change sides—any way that suited the other man would suit him—any way just so's he got a bet, he was satisfied. But still, he was lucky—uncommon lucky; he most always come out winner. He was always ready and laying for a chance; there couldn't be no solitry thing mentioned but that feller'd offer to bet on it—and take any side you please, as I was just telling you. If there was a horse-race, you'd find him flush, or you'd find him busted at the end of it; if there was a dog-fight, he'd bet on it; if there was a cat-fight, he'd bet on it; if there was a chicken-fight, he'd bet on it; why, if there was two birds setting on a fence, he would bet you which one would fly first—or if there was a camp-meeting, he would be there reglar, to bet on Parson Walker, which he judged to be the best exhorter about here, and so he was, too, and a good man. If he even seen a straddle-bug start to go any wheres, he would bet you how long it would take him to get wherever he was going to, and if you took him up, he would foller that straddle-bug to Mexico but what he would find out where he was bound for and how long he was on the road. Lots of the boys here has seen that Smiley, and can tell you about him. Why, it never made no difference to him—he would bet on anything—the dangdest feller. Parson Walker's wife laid very sick, once, for a good while, and it seemed as if they wam't going to save her; but one morning he come in, and Smiley asked him how she was, and he said she was considerable better—thank the Lord for his inf'nit mercy—and coming on so smart that, with the blessing of Providence, she'd get well yet—and Smiley, before he thought, says, "Well, I'll resk two-and-a-half that she don't, anyway."

Thish-yer Smiley had a mare—the boys called her the fifteen-minute nag, but that was only in fun, you know, because, of course, she was faster than that—and he used to win money on that horse, for all she was so slow and always had the asthma, or the distemper, or the consumption, or something of that kind. They used to give her two or three hundred yards' start, and then pass her under way; but always at the fag-end of the race she'd get excited and desperate-like, and come cavorting and straddling up, and scattering her legs around limber, sometimes in the air, and sometimes out to one side amongst the fences, and kicking up m-o-r-e dust, and raising m-o-r-e racket with her coughing and sneezing and blowing her nose—and always fetch up at the stand just about a neck ahead, as near as you could cipher it down.

And he had a little small buff pup, that to look at him you'd think he warn't worth a cent, but to set around and look ornery, and lay for a chance to steal something. But as soon as money was up on him, he was a different dog—his underjaw'd begin to stick out like the fo'castle of a steamboat, and his teeth would uncover, and shine savage like the furnaces. And a dog might tackle him, and bully-rag him, and bite him, and throw him over his shoulder two or three times, and Andrew Jackson—which was the name of the pup—Andrew Jackson would never let on but what he was satisfied, and hadn't expected nothing else—and the bets being doubled and doubled on the other side all the time, till the money was all up—and then all of a sudden he would grab that other dog jest by the j'int of his hind leg and freeze to it—not chaw, you understand, but only jest grip and hang on till they thronged up the sponge, if it was a year. Smiley always come out winner on that pup, till he harnessed a dog once that didn't have no hind legs, because they'd been sawed off in a circular saw, and when the thing had gone along far enough, and the money was all up, and he come to make a snatch for his pet holt, he saw in a minute how he'd been imposed on, and how the other dog had him in the door, so to speak, and he 'peared surprised, and then he looked sorter discouraged-like, and didn't try no more to win the fight, and so he got shucked out bad. He give Smiley a look, as much as to say his heart was broke, and it was his fault, for putting up a dog that hadn't no hind legs for him to take holt of, which was his main dependence in a fight, and then he limped off a piece and laid down and died. It was a good pup, was that Andrew Jackson, and would have made a name for hisself if he'd lived, for the stuff was in him, and he had genius—I know it, because he hadn't had no opportunities to speak of, and it don't stand to reason that a dog could make such a fight as he could under them circumstances, if he hadn't no talent. It always makes me feel sorry when I think of that last fight of his'n, and the way it turned out.

    Well, thish-yer Smiley had rat-tarriers, and chicken cocks, and tom-cats, and all of them kind of things, till you couldn't rest, and you couldn't fetch nothing for him to bet on but he'd match you. He ketched a frog one day, and took him home, and said he cal'klated to edercate him; and so he never done nothing for three months but set in his back yard and learn that frog to jump. And you bet you he did learn him, too. He'd give him a little hunch behind, and the next minute you'd see that frog whirling in the air like a doughnut—see him turn one summerset, or may be a couple, if he got a good start, and come down flat-footed and all right, like a cat. He got him up so in the matter of ketching flies, and kept him in practice so constant, that he'd nail a fly every time as far as he could see him. Smiley said all a frog wanted was education, and he could do most anything—and I believe him.

Why, I've seen him set Dan'l Webster down here on this floor—Dan'l Webster was the name of the frog—and sing out, "Flies, Dan'l, flies!" and quicker'n you could wink, he'd spring straight up, and snake a fly off'n the counter there, and flop down on the floor again as solid as a gob of mud, and fall to scratching the side of his head with his hind foot as indifferent as if he hadn't no idea he'd been doin' any more'n any frog might do. You never see a frog so modest and straightfor'ard as he was, for all he was so gifted. And when it come to fair-and-square jumping on a dead level, he could get over more ground at one straddle than any animal of his breed you ever see. Jumping on a dead level was his strong suit, you understand, and when it come to that, Smiley would ante up money on him as long as he had a red. Smiley was monstrous proud of his frog, and well he might be, for fellers that had traveled and ben everywheres, all said he laid over any frog that ever they see.

Well, Smiley kept the beast in a little lattice box, and he used to fetch him down town sometimes and lay for a bet. One day a feller—a stranger in the camp, he was—come across him with his box, and says:

"What might it be that you've got in the box?"

And Smiley says, sorter indifferent like, "It might be a parrot, or it might be a canary, may be, but it ain't—it's only just a frog."

And the feller took it, and looked at it careful, and turned it round this way and that, and says, "H'm—so 'tis. Well, what's he good for?"

"Well," Smiley says, easy and careless, "He's good enough for one thing, I should judge—he can out-jump ary frog in Calaveras county."

The feller took the box again, and took another long, particular look, and give it back to Smiley, and says, very deliberate, "Well—I don't see no p'ints about that frog that's any better'n any other frog."

"Maybe you don't," Smiley says. "Maybe you understand frogs, and maybe you don't understand 'em; maybe you've had experience, and maybe you ain't only a amature, as it were. Anyways, I've got my opinion, and I'll resk forty dollars that he can out-jump any frog in Calaveras county."

And the feller studied a minute, and then says, kinder sad, like, "Well, I'm only a stranger here, and I ain't got no frog—but if I had a frog, I'd bet you."

And then Smiley says, "That's all right—that's all right—if you'll hold my box a minute, I'll go and get you a frog." And so the feller took the box, and put up his forty dollars along with Smiley's, and set down to wait.

So he set there a good while thinking and thinking to hisself, and then he got the frog out and prized his mouth open and took a tea-spoon and filled him full of quail shot—filled him pretty near up to his chin—and set him on the floor. Smiley he went to the swamp and slopped around in the mud for a long time, and finally he ketched a frog, and fetched him in, and give him to this feller, and says:

"Now if you're ready, set him alongside of Dan'l, with his fore-paws just even with Dan'l's, and I'll give the word." Then he says, "One—two—three—jump!" and him and the feller touched up the frogs from behind, and the new frog hopped off, but Dan'l give a heave, and hysted up his shoulders—so—like a Frenchman, but it wasn't no use—he couldn't budge; he was planted as solid as an anvil, and he couldn't no more stir than if he was anchored out. Smiley was a good deal surprised, and he was disgusted too, but he didn't have no idea what the matter was, of course.

The feller took the money and started away; and when he was going out at the door, he sorter jerked his thumb over his shoulders—this way—at Dan'l, and says again, very deliberate, "Well, I don't see no p'ints about that frog that's any better'n any other frog."

Smiley he stood scratching his head and looking down at Dan'l a long time, and at last he says, "I do wonder what in the nation that frog throw'd off for—I wonder if there ain't something the matter with him—he 'pears to look mighty baggy, somehow"—and he ketched Dan'l by the nap of the neck, and lifted him up and says, "Why, blame my cats, if he don't weigh five pound!"—and turned him upside down, and he belched out a double-handful of shot. And then he see how it was, and he was the maddest man—he set the frog down and took out after that feller, but he never ketchd him. And—

[Here Simon Wheeler heard his name called from the front yard, and got up to go and see what was wanted.] And turning to me as he moved away, he said: "Just set where you are, stranger, and rest easy—I ain't going to be gone a second."

But, by your leave, I did not think that a continuation of the history of the enterprising vagabond Jim Smiley would be likely to afford me much information concerning the Rev. Leonidas W. Smiley, and so I started away.

At the door I met the sociable Wheeler returning, and he button-holed me and recommenced:

"Well, thish-yer Smiley had a yeller one-eyed cow that didn't have no tail, only jest a short stump like a bannanner, and"

"O, curse Smiley and his afflicted cow!" I muttered, good-naturedly, and bidding the old gentleman good-day, I departed.

3

Eric Blair

The classic novel, *1984*, is an horrific dystopian view of the world circa 1948; perhaps the most horrific novel *of any kind* ever published. Many of the terms in the novel are now universal:

> Big Brother ... Big Brother is Watching You ... Doublethink ... Thought Crime ... Memory Hole ... Telescreen ... Newspeak ... Thought Police ... War is Peace; Freedom is Slavery; Ignorance is Strength ...

... and now ...

> ... Orwellian

... which describes any authoritarian or totalitarian government.

Like Samuel Langhorne Clemens, Eric Blair—born June 2, 1903 and died Jan. 21, 1950—had world experiences fundamental to his writing. He was born in India, to a family genteel but not wealthy. His father worked in the India Civil Service. A year after he was born his mother took him and his two sisters to live in England, presumably for a better life. Blair saw his father briefly in 1907, when his father was on leave, but not again until 1912. Blair's school years were abysmal. He hated his first school, St. Cyrian's, in East Sussex. He described his next school, Wellington, as "beastly," but apparently was happier at Eton.

Financially he couldn't afford further university work without scholarship help, which didn't look promising; he thus decided to leave England. In October, 1922, he traveled through the Suez Canal and Ceylon and arrived in Rangoon in November, to join the Indian Imperial Police. He was posted in the Irrawaddy Delta area, then closer to Rangoon.

He gained responsibility there quite young; while his contemporaries in England were still in school. He learned the Burmese language but contracted dengue fever in 1927. He took leave and returned to England, examined his life and resigned from the Indian Imperial Police to become a writer.

Like Clemens before him, he mined his travel experiences; his novel *Burmese Days* was published in 1934.

Later, in 1927 he moved to London. He had previously admired the work of Jack London; for his next project, he changed his appearance, dressed like a tramp, changed his name to P.S. Burton and explored the lives of the lower class. In 1928, he moved to Paris and lived in a working class district. He began writing an early version of *Burmese Days* there. He wrote short pieces: on unemployment; a day in the life of a tramp and the beggars of London. He became obsessed with poverty and was—during those times—often close to it himself. He worked as a dishwasher and took menial odd jobs. He became seriously ill in February, 1929, and was taken to a charity hospital.

He spent two years in Paris and eventually published *Down and Out in Paris and London* (1933).

But he was no longer Eric Blair—he wanted no connection with his colonial British policeman's past and wanted no connection to his education at Eton. He considered four pseudonyms: P.S. Burton, his tramp name; Kenneth Miles; George Orwell and H. Lewis Allways. He settled on Orwell. He *became* George Orwell. Anonymous. A cipher. Orwell, perhaps from the Orwell River that runs through Suffolk. As Orwell, he could expose the corruption of the British colonial system in *Burmese Days* and could also expose injustices he saw in England and Europe.

Both *Burmese Days* and *Down and Out in Paris and London* were published under the pseudonym George Orwell.

British publisher Victor Gollancz, was establishing a publishing house specializing in left-wing titles, specifically pacifistic and socialistic non-fiction He also launched the Left Book Club. In early 1936, he urged Orwell to investigate conditions in economically-depressed northern England. In late January, Orwell reached Manchester. He interviewed citizens there, collected data on living conditions and wages, and conditions in local coal mines.

He published *The Road to Wigan Pier* in 1937: it was a mixed work. The first half consists of his reportage from the Manchester area; the second half, a very extended essay on his developing liberal philosophy, which included an argument for

Socialism as he saw it. Gollancz feared the second half would offend readers who approved of the thrust of his publishing house. Gollancz subsequently added a Preface, while Orwell was in Spain fighting in the Spanish Civil War. Gallancz's Preface separated himself and his publishing house from Orwell's opinions in the book.

Orwell's reportage from northern England resulted in him being placed under surveillance by the British government from 1936 to 1948, one year before the publication of *1984*.

Orwell married Eileen O'Shaughnessy June 9, 1936. Soon thereafter the crises began that would lead to the Spanish Civil War. Orwell followed those developments avidly. He decided to go to Spain and fight on the Republican side, against Franco and Hitler's legions, sent as a rehearsal for a later war.

He traveled to Spain December 23, 1936 and found almost impossible situations there; the Republican side was rife with factions, including Marxist groups and the Unified Socialist party, which distrusted each other.

He was sent to the Aragon front in January 1937 but in April was back in Barcelona; again sent to the front he was hit in the throat by a sniper; blood poured from his throat and he was barely able to speak. He received electrotheraphy and was deemed unfit for further service. His time in the Spanish Civil War was over.

Back in England, his health again collapsed. In March 1938, he was admitted to the Preston Hall Sanatorium, in Kent and diagnosed—initially—with tuberculosis.

Homage to Catalonia was published in 1938 by Seeker and Warburg (not by Gollancz his previous publisher). It did not succeed.

He and his wife journeyed to French Morocco in September, 1938, where, it was thought, the climate might be better for his health. He wrote *Coming Up for Air* there.

Jump forward in time to the war years.

In many respects, Orwell himself did not have a very good war. "They won't have in the army, at any rate at present, because of my lungs," he told a friend. That's no surprise. In a 1938 medical examination, he was found to stand six feet three and to weight just 159 pounds, and an X-ray slide showed shadows on his lungs. Despite that, and despite his neck wound, he remained a heavy smoker of strong hand-rolled cigarettes. He was again unlucky when he sought work at the Air Ministry's public relations office. Meanwhile, his wife was working at a government censorship office.

In his article, "Honest Decent, Wrong: the invention of George Orwell," Louis Menard writes:

> During the war, Orwell took a job with the India section of the BBC's Eastern Service, where he produced and, with T.S. Eliot, William Empson, Louis MacNeice and other distinguished writers, delivered radio talks, mostly on literary subjects, intended to rally the support of Indians for he British war effort. For the first time since 1927, he received the salary he had once enjoyed as a policeman in Burma, but he regarded the work as propaganda—he felt, he said,

like "an orange that's been trodden on by a very dirty boot."—and, in 1943, he quit He worked for a while as literary editor and as a columnist at the *Tribune*, a Social paper edited by Aneuerin Bevan, the leader of the left wing of the Labour Party in Britain and a man Orwell admired.

His wife, Eileen, entered a hospital March 29, 1945, for a routine operation to remove uterine tumors, but she died under the anesthetic. His subsequent death, alone and 46 was tragic; her death was equally tragic. When she died, she was not yet 40.

His next book, written between November i943 and February 1944, brought him international fame—it was, in fact, a perfect combination of propaganda and art, philosophy and fable: *Animal Farm*, first published in 1945.

The plot: most of the animals on the Manor Farm have names (Just as in Clement Clark Moore's "'Twas the Night Before Christmas"—*on Dasher, on Dancer, on Prancer and Vixen …*")

And how did Orwell conceive of the plot for this, which can be read both as a fable and a cautionary political tale? A leap of insight which writers sometimes find to their great benefit—and often to their surprise. In the Preface, Orwell writes:

> … I saw a little boy, perhaps ten years old, driving a huge carthorse along a narrow path, whipping it whenever it tried to turn. It stuck me that if only such animals became aware of their strength we should have no power over them and that men exploit

animals in much the same way as the rich exploit the proletariat.

And an even earlier genesis of *Animal Farm* as fable is his memory of his favorite book as a child:

> I believe *Gulliver's Travels* has meant more to me than any other book ever written. I can't remember when I first read it. I must have been eight years old at the most, and it has lived with me ever since so that I suppose a year has never passed without my re-reading at least part of it.

On the farm, Old Major, an old boar summons the animals together for a meeting in which he refers to humans as "enemies." They all learn a revolutionary song "Beasts of England." When he dies, two young pigs Snowball and Napoleon become leaders and prepare others for a coming revolution. They force the drunken farmer Mr. Jones from the farm and rename it Animal Farm. They adopt a dictum: the "Seven Commandments of Animalism."

The seven were:

1. Whatever goes upon two legs is an enemy.
2. Whatever goes upon four legs, or has wings, is a friend.
3. No animals shall wear clothes.
4. No animal shall sleep in a bed.
5. No animal shall drink alcohol.

> 6. No animal shall kill any other animal.
> 7. All animals are equal.

The most important was: *All animals are equal.*
It becomes a commune.

Later the farmer and other humans attempt to recapture the farm; they are driven away and the victory is celebrated annually as "The Battle of the Cowshed."

The honesty and trust among the animals beings to fray: Snowball announces his plan to build a windmill, but Napoleon has his dogs chase Snowball away and he declares himself leader of Animal Farm. He has others chased away as well. When some remember "The Battle of Cowshed," Napoleon, who was nowhere to be seen during the battle, replaces the song "Beasts of England," with a song that glorifies him. Eventually the windmill is destroyed by a storm; it was rebuilt, but was destroyed again by another attack by humans.

Eventually the idealistic communal plans that Snowball discussed are forgotten. The pigs begin to appear human-like. The original Seven Commandments including "All animals are equal" had been changed by Napoleon:

> 4. No animal shall sleep in a bed *with sheets.*
> 5. No animal shall drink alcohol *to excess.*
> 6. No animal shall kill another animal *without cause.*

But all the Commandments were eventually replaced by a single line:

> *All animals are equal but some animals are more equal than others.*

Orwell intended *Animal Farm* to be an attack on the dictatorship and brutal practices in the Stalinist years in Russia, based on what he saw during the Spanish Civil War and what he knew about communism under Stalin.

Animal Farm received decidedly mixed reviews when it was first published; now decades away from the Stalinist years in Russia, critics have said eventually every part—every incident and anecdote—of the book had a parallel in that period of political history.

It has become a classic: part propaganda, part art; part allegory, part political philosophy.

Orwell's masterwork: *1984*

Then came Orwell's masterwork: *1984*. (The original title was *Nineteen Eighty-Four*, but many editions since have titled it simply *1984*, which we are using here.)

For journalists, an article beginning is called the *lede* (pronounced *leed*). Orwell's lede in *1984* is one of the most memorable in literature:

> It was a bright cold day in April, and the clocks were striking thirteen.

In *1984*, there are three world powers, constantly at war with each other: Eastasia, China and smaller satellite countries;

Eurasia, the Soviet Union and Oceania, the United States, the United Kingdom and their allies.

In London, Winston Smith is a minor functionary, working for the Party. Surveillance is constant. The Party's leader Big Brother is on billboards and everywhere else. The slogan *Big Brother is Watching* You is everywhere. There is no escaping The Party or Big Brother.

The Party prohibits free expression, free thought, any effort to be an individual and even prohibits sex. The Party has crafted its own history and is working to implement a new language *Newspeak; bad* is now *not good*. If the party can control language it can control history and behavior.

Smith works at Ministry of Truth, which works on historical revisionism; changing history to reflect the party line. Revisions are explained as fixing misquotations, but are in fact outright lies and forgeries. The Ministry of Truth destroys historical documents; if a document does not exist, there is no proof The Party is lying.

Smith knows how the Ministry of Truth is distorting history; he lives a shabby life in "Victory Mansions," subsisting on black bread, synthetic meals and "Victory" gin.

Telescreens are everywhere—flat screens which can observe everyone and anyone; especially those who might challenge the party's authority. Even children are encouraged by the party to inform on their parents relatives or friends.

There is virtually no escape from the constant surveillance of The Party.

Everything about The Party is a black reversal:

The Ministry of Peace deals with war;

The Ministry of Plenty deals with starvation;

The Ministry of Love deals with law and order, which means torture and brainwashing;

The Ministry of Truth deals with propaganda.

Wilson begins writing a journal, which he knows is a death warrant. He records his feelings about Julia, a worker aiso in his office complex.

Julia subsequently hands him a note—she is in love with him. They meet upstairs above an antique shop, where Smith bought his journal They assume there are no telescreens in the old, shabby building. But they are betrayed by the owner of the shop, who is a member of the Thought Police.

Smith is taken to the Ministry of Love, He is interrogated by O'Brien, who Smith knows, a member of the party, in a position slightly above Smith.

O'Brien subjects Smith to electroshock treatments and tells Smith that he can be "cured" of his '"insanity'—his hatred of the Party—through conditioning. Smith confesses to "crimes" he has committed.

He is eventually taken to Room 101—the ultimate location of re-indoctrination—brainwashing.

It is every citizen's worst fear about The Party.

Smith betrays Julia when a wire cage with live rats inside is fitted over his head.

"Do it to Julia," he says, in abject panic.

He later meets Julia on the street, in a crowd—she admits she betrayed him, in Room 101, faced with the same wire cage with the hungry rats.

Eventually he is content to sit in a cafe, remembering a rare happy time with his family, but now believes it to be false.

He is fully content to love Big Brother.

Neologisms in *1984* ...

More than the plot, Orwell's portraits of the ultimate authoritarian or totalitarian state and his neologisms—newly coined words or phrases—have made *1984* the timeless classic that it remains today.

They include:

- *Big Brother.* The most memorable image from the book.

How did he create Big Brother? A simple explanation is that a British company advertising correspondence courses used billboards with a kindly looking J.M. Bennett, the company owner, with the phrase "Let me be your father." When he died, his son took over the business and the billboards then carried the line, "Let me be your big brother."

Another surmise is that Big Brother was a Stalinesque figure.

A third surmise is that Orwell worked in the B.B.C. during World War Two, with Brendan Bracken, the British Minister of Information—initials B.B.

Orwell also admitted that propaganda by the British during World War Two (which he helped produce) was at least partially a source for his description of totalitarian propaganda in *1984*.

- *Thought Police.* Any independent thinking which reflected against The Party could be pursued as a *thoughtcrime.*
- *Doublethink.* The ability to believe in two sides of an issue at the same time.

Trump spokesman Sean Spicer said, after the Trump inaugural, "The Trump inaugural crowds were the biggest ever. Period." When reporters and TV networks produced aerial photographs showing that the first Obama inaugural had far, far more spectators, Trump spokesman Kellyanne Conway said that Spicer was stating "alternative facts." That phrase, *alternative facts,* would be appropriate on any page of *1984.*

- *Room 101.* The ultimate torture chamber for Party non-believers. Orwell worked in a room 101 when he was with the B.B.C. during World War Two.
- *Newspeak.* The party's revisions of the common language. Who controls language controls facts, truth, the past and the public.
- *Memory Hole.* When the past is obliterated from history; when the past no longer exists, it goes down the *memory hole.*
- *Telescreen.* Flat, wall-mounted screens in every home and apartment; the Party can view *into* homes and apartments constantly. Residents who wish to talk freely must hide in a corner away from the viewing area of the *telescreen* or talk outside.

- *Unperson.* A person whose name and history has been obliterated from history. Completely.

Aftermath …

Previously, Orwell and his wife had adopted a child, a son, Richard. Orwell's flat had been damaged by a Nazi rocket, and … eventually he was diagnosed with tuberculosis.

Jura was, perhaps, the least likely place for Orwell to complete his novel. Located in the Inner Hebrides of Scotland … Jura is mountainous, bare and infertile, covered largely by vast area of blanket bog, hence its small population. In a list of the islands of Scotland, ranked by size Jura comes in eighth, whereas by population it comes in thirty-first. Jura, in ancient Norse, means Deer Island.

The house in Jura (biographer Jeffrey Meyers calls this his "Jurassic Period") was scarcely more than a place to live and to finish *1984*.

Robert McCrum tells the rest of the story in his article, "1984: The masterpiece that killed George Orwell":

Orwell had worked for David Astor, publisher of *The Observer*. Astor offered him a place to stay:

> His family owned an estate on the remote Scottish island of Jura next to Islay. There was a house,

Barnhill, seven miles outside Ardlussa at the remote northern tip off this rocky finger of heather in the Inner Hebrides. Initially Astor offered it to Orwell as a holiday.

In May, 1946 Orwell, still picking up the shattered pieces of his life, took the train for the long and arduous journey to Jura. He told his friend Arthur Koestler that it was "almost like stocking up ship for an arctic voyage."

The residents knew him by his real name: Eric Blair, "a tall cadaverous, sad-looking man worrying about how to cope on his own ... a spectre in the mist, a gaunt figure in oilskins." His sister Avril then arrived to manage things. It was a godsend to Orwell.

Then, an accident—a disaster for Orwell. In a boat with Arvil, Richard and some friends, a infamous whirlpool capsized the boat. Son Richard remembered being "bloody cold."

But Orwell went on with his manuscript. Within two months he was seriously ill, but he still kept on. At Christmas, 1947, he told friends that he had been diagnosed with tuberculosis. Then, in March, 1948, he received word from his publisher Fred Warburg: "it's necessary from the point of view of your literary career to get it (done) by the end of the year and indeed earlier if possible."

Get it done by the end of 1948. Or sooner. While fighting tuberculosis.

TIMELESS (PEN) NAMES

Robert McCrum writes:

It was a desperate race against time. Orwell's health wras deteriorating, the "unbelievable bad" manuscript needed retyping, and the December deadline was looming. Warburg promised to help, as did Orwell's agent. At cross-purposes over possible typists, they somehow contrived to make a bad situation infinitely worse. Orwell, feeling beyond help, followed his ex-public schoolboy's instincts: he would go it alone.

The manuscript reached Orwell's publisher in mid-December. Fred Warburg recognized its importance immediately: "among the most terrifying books I have ever read."

Orwell entered a TB sanitarium.

1984 was published June 8, 1949 and was instantly recognized as a masterpiece. Winston Churchill said he had read it—twice.

In October, 1949, in his room at University College Hospital, Orwell married Sonia Brownell. It was a moment of happiness—but only a fleeting moment.

Orwell suffered a massive hemorrhage January 15, 1950. He died alone, at 46.

In *Churchill and Orwell: The Fight for Freedom*, Thomas E. Ricks writes: "When he was alive, his book sales were measured in the hundreds and thousands. Since his death an estimated 50 million copies of his books have been sold."

And, Ricks states:

In the post 9/11 era, 1984 particularly has found a new relevance, and a new generation of Westerns readers ...

For present-day Americans, *1984*'s background of permanent warfare carries a chilling warning. In the book, as in American life today, the conflict is offstage, heard only as occasional rocket impacts in the distance. "Winston could not definitely remember a time when his country has not been at war," Orwell stated in *1984*. (The same is true of all Americans now in their early twenties or younger. In the novel, some even suspect the government is faking the war, claiming one is under way in order to maintain its hold on power.)

In an era when American wars are waged with drones firing precision-guided missiles, and with small numbers of Navy SEALs and other Special Operations Forces on the ground in remote parts of the Middle East, with occasional enemy bombings in cities such as London, Paris, Madrid and New York, this passage from the novel is eerily prescient:

It is a warfare of limited aims between combatants who are unable to destroy one another, (and) have no material cause for fighting . . .(it) involves very small numbers of people, mostly highly trained specialists, and causes comparatively few casualties. The fighting, when there is any, takes place on the vague frontiers whose whereabouts the average man can only guess at. In the centers of civilization war means no more than . . . the occasional crash of a rocket bomb which may cause a few scores of deaths.

from *1984*

It was a bright cold day in April, and the clocks were striking thirteen. Winston Smith, his chin muzzled into his breast in an effort to escape the vile wind, slipped quickly through the glass doors of Victory Mansions though not quickly enough to prevent a swirl of gritty dust from entering along with him.

The hallway smelt of boiled cabbage and old rag mats. At one end of it a colored poster, far too large for indoor display, had been tacked to the wall. It depicted simply an enormous face, more than a meter wide; the face of a man about forty-five, with a heavy black mustache and ruggedly handsome features. Winston made for the stairs. It was no use trying the lift. Even at the best of times it was seldom working and at present the electric current was cut off during daylight hours. It was part of the economy drive in preparation for Hate Week.

* * *

The Ministry of Truth—Minitrue in Newspeak—was startlingly different from any other object in sight. It was an enormous pyramidal structure of glittering white concrete, soaring up terrace after terrace, three hundred meters into the air. From where Winston stood it was just possible to read, picked out on its white face in elegant lettering, the three slogans of the Party:

    WAR IS PEACE
    FREEDOM IS SLAVERY
    IGNORANCE IS STRENGTH

4

Theodor Geisel

"He was …" *Time* magazine wrote in a feature obituary after his death, "one of the last doctors to make house calls—some 200 million of them in 20 languages. By the time of his death last week at 87, Dr. Seuss had journeyed on beyond Dr. Spook to a unique and hallowed place in the nurseries of the world."

Theodor "Ted" Seuss Geisel (March 2, 1904–September 24, 1991) was born in Springfield, Massachusetts which, at that time, seems idyllic—even quaint. There was family names like Wickersham, Terwilliger and McElligot, which he would use later in his books.

The Geisels (pronounced GUY-sell) were German and there was a large German community of about a thousand—to twelve hundred—in Springfield. But there were three events in Ted Geisel's early life that would be memorable:

- In 1907, when Ted Geisel was three, a sister, Marnie, named after his mother, died of pneumonia in their home. Geisel was haunted hearing the "terrible sounds of her cough." Her little coffin was displayed in the house. Late the family owned a "Pooley cabinet"; a narrow New England-made cabinet in which his father kept Caruso records. Ted Geisel was haunted again by the similarity of the Pooley cabinet to the small coffin which had held his sister. His only reaction to her death: a stoic silence.

- In 1914, America entered The Great War—World War One. As German-Americans, the Geisel family faced considerable hostility. Sauerkraut was renamed "victory cabbage" frankfurters became hot dogs. The Geisels were suspect in their own community. They spoke German at home, ate bratwurst and drank beer. Ted Geisel often wondered why they were suddenly *the other* ...
- Worse, Geisel's grandfather—also known as Theodor Geisel, along with a partner, Christian Kalmbach had begun a brewery, Kalmbach and Geisel, which everyone called *Come Back and Guzzle.* Eventually it became one of the largest breweries in New England—it grew and merged and became Liberty Breweries—with, at one time, twenty-five matching horses to pull black and gold brewery wagons through the streets.

But Prohibition began in 1920 (and ended in 1933) and that put *Come Back and Guzzle*—out of business.

Geisel's father who had been with the brewery, joined the Springfield Park Board, which included the Springfield Zoo.

Ted Geisel ...

TIMESLESS (PEN) NAMES

> … took a pencil and pad to the Zoo and began to draw the animals that he saw. But his animals were awkward, misshapen and, well, tended toward the bizarre. Any normal parents inspecting the drawings of a precocious child might reasonably expect that the drawings would become more accurate and realistic over time and the experiences and age of the child. Ted Geisel's animals remained awkward, mis-shapen and bizarre. Over the years, he *sharpened his skill at making them awkward, misshapen and bizarre.*

This became an accident of great fortune, although Ted Geisel may have been too young to clearly understand it at the time.

One of his first and sustaining memories was playing with lion cubs … and … he could hear, from his bedroom window, the night sounds of the animals at the Zoo.

Years later he could remember the rainbow colors of the Victorian homes in Springfield, and the sounds and smells of the Zoo animals.

He was also fascinated by the comics—his father brought a newspaper home every night and Ted was influenced by "Crazy Kat" and other comic strips of the time.

He had to take an art class in Springfield's Central High School in the fall of 1917. He later explained what happened:

> Our model that day was a milk bottle containing a few scraggly late autumn daisies. I was having a real bad time trying to capture the beauty of this set-up and immortalize it with a hunk of charcoal and a

sheet of paper. To add to my frustration, my teacher kept fluttering about and giving me hell for turning my drawing board around and working on my picture upside down. "No Theodor," she said, "Not upside down. There are rules that every artist must abide by. You will never succeed if you break them."

Geisel transferred out of that class.
We can almost hear it later as a typical Dr. Seuss rhyme:

> *No Theodor, No Theodor,*
> *Not upside down, not upside down,*
> *Not even once, not evermore …*
> *This I implore, not evermore …*

Geisel was doing as other youngsters always do—he was creating a world with no rules. Why shouldn't you, *why shouldn't you, draw upside down?* He was also drawing from the right side of his brain, and making perfect sense while doing so. And when he acknowledged to himself that he would take no more art-by-the-books classes, he permanently freed himself from any further *not upside down* rules. (The same exact incident once happened to James Thurber.)

After graduating from high school, Geisel decided to attend Dartmouth, because a favorite teacher had gone there. The tuition in the fall of 1921: $250 annually. He had no special interest in fraternities, but was surprised when no fraternity pledged him. He discovered why: with a sharp nose and black hair, the fraternities thought him Jewish. He turned to the campus humor magazine, the *Jack-o-Lantern*, which staffers called the *Jacko*. He was a natural.

And, in the words of a college friend, Frederick "Pete" Blodgett:

> He never had any money but he never spent much. He was always raising hell and laughing a lot and didn't study worth a damn.

It was popular—and cynical—for the Dartmouth students to exclaim: "Oh! The places you'll go! The people you'll meet!"

Over six decades later, in 1990, Dr. Seuss published *Oh! The Places You'll Go!* which became favorite high school and college graduation gifts.

In his senior year he was elected to Casque and Gauntlet, the Dartmouth senior honorary society. One member, Kenneth Montgomery, remembered Geisel:

> He was not gregarious in the sense of hail-fellow-well-met; there was no sense of self-importance about him. Burt when he walked into a room it was like a magician's act. Birds flew out of his hands, and less bright scarves and fireworks. Everything became brighter, happier, funnier. And he didn't try. Everything Ted did seemed to be a surprise, even to him.

In April, 1925, he was caught with some bootleg liquor. The Dartmouth Dean demanded that he write his parents telling them that he was on probation. He was also forbidden to contribute to the *Jack-o-Lantern,* but not banned from their offices. So he continued to contribute to the magazine, using a variety of pen names including Sing Sing, the name of the New York state penitentiary and—he also used Seuss.

Seuss was his mother's maiden name and his middle name. Since it was German, it should be pronounced *Zoice,* but non-German speakers wouldn't know that, so *Zioce* quickly—and universally—was pronounced *Seuss.* Later he added *Dr.* because his father wanted him to either complete a doctorate or practice medicine.

When he was due to graduate from Dartmouth, he had no plans—no career, no job in sight. Back home, his father asked him what he plans were—what he was going to do. Geisel impulsively said he was going to win a Campbell Scholarship from Dartmouth to go to Oxford. Oxford. In England. That Oxford. But it wasn't true; he *had* applied for the scholarship, but didn't get it.

Before he could explain all that to his father, his father told the editor of *The Springfield Union* newspaper, who happened to live across the street from the Geisels. Ted Geisel remembered it was on the front page:

GEISEL WINS FELLOWSHIP TO GO TO OXFORD

When he finally told his father that he hadn't received the scholarship, he was met with cold silence; the silence was overwhelming. His father finally said that if Ted announced he would go to Oxford, he would go—friends and family would eventually forget the scholarship.

And so he went.

He majored there, in English and writing. But ruefully said:

> English and writing was my major, but I think that's a mistake for anybody. That's teaching you the mechanics of getting water out of a well that may not exist.

True advice, ignored by thousands of English majors everywhere.

Again, he was the outsider; he was a Yank in a British university and he was of German extraction in a country which had not yet forgotten World War One.

He found Oxford life trivial, tedious or bizarre. And pompous. Very pompous. It had centuries of pomposity to live up to. Geisel was alternatively bemused or leery of it all. He attended lectures on Geoffrey Chaucer, who he called Jeff and doodled in the margins of his notebooks. Supremely bored by it all.

Then he met Helen Marion Palmer, who had graduated from Wellesley and had taught English for three years in Brooklyn before coming to Oxford.

Their first encounter: Geisel had—in his own way—illustrated great chucks of *Paradise Lost*.

> With the imagery of *Paradise Lost* Milton's sense of humor failed him in a couple of places. I remember one line, "Thither came the angel Uriel, sliding down a sunbeam."

I illustrated that: Uriel had a long locomotive oil can and was greasing the sunbeam as he descended, to lessen the friction on his coccyx.

"You're crazy to be a professor," (Helen) said, after a class.

"What you really want to do is draw," and said, looking at his sketchbook, "that's a very fine flying cow."

She had picked him up.

Any woman who could appreciate Uriel and his oil can, and a flying cow and a drooling cow with a sagging udder, a Chaplinesque clown, dogs walking on high wires, a chicken with a windmill for a tail—that woman was for him.

He quickly fell in love with her and she, just as quickly, fell in love with him.

He was at the verge of giving up on Oxford. He and Helen spent some time in Europe—touring Switzerland, Munich, Nuremberg, Dresden and Berlin. In the village of Kleinschwarzenbach, they hosted a party for Seuss family members and 67 people attended.

He returned to Oxford and gave it one more try. It was useless. He returned to the United States in February 1927. Once again he had no job, no prospects for a job, *no talent for a job*. And no degree from Oxford. He retreated to his father's desk and again drew the odd, mis-shapen bizarre animals he had drawn before. They weren't frightening, just odd.

He journeyed to New York City, where he later said:

> I have tramped all over this bloody town and been tossed out of Boni and Liveright (publishing house), Harcourt Brace, Paramount Pictures, three advertising agencies, *Life*, *Judge* (magazine) and three public conveniences …

Finally one day he got an envelope from *The Saturday Evening Post*. He had submitted a cartoon of *two* American tourists riding camels and comparing themselves to Lawrence of Arabia. *The Post* bought it for $25. He had signed it: Seuss.

On that thin Seuss success, he moved to New York and got a job at the humor magazine *Judge*, for $75 a *week*. On that salary he and Helen could get married, which they did November 29, 1927.

Shortly later he added *Dr.* to his pseudonym, because, he said, it made up for the doctoral degree he never got at Oxford and, he said, he wanted to use his own name for the Great American Novel he wanted to write. It was a dream; he never wrote that novel and never used his own name in print.

He always claimed that serendipity played a large part in his career. *Judge* was faltering as a magazine, but a financial windfall soon occurred. He said, later …

> I'd been working for *Judge* about four months when I drew this accidental cartoon which changed my whole life. It was an insect gag.
>
> It was a picture of a knight who had gone to bed He had stacked his armor beside the bed. Here was

this covered canopy over the bed, and a tremendous dragon was sort of nuzzling him.

He looked up and said, "Darn it all, Another dragon. And just when I'd sprayed the whole castle with …"

With what? I wondered.

There were two well known insecticides. One was Flit and the other Fly-Tox. So I tossed a coin. It came up heads, for Flit.

So, the caption read "… another dragon. And just after I sprayed the whole castle with Flit."

Here's where luck comes in.

Very few people read *Judge*. It was continually in bankruptcy—and everybody else was bankrupt too.

But one day the wife of Lincoln L. Cleaves, who was the account executive at the McCann-Erickson advertising agency failed to get an appointment at her favorite hairdresser's, and went to a second-rate hairdresser's, where they had second-rate magazines.

She opened *Judge* while waiting to get her hair dressed, and she found this picture. She ripped it out of the magazine, put it in her reticule, took it home, bearded her husband with it, and said, "Lincoln, you've got to hire this young man; it's the best Flit ad I've ever seen."

He said, "Go away." He said, "You're my wife and you're to have nothing to do with my business."

So she finally pestered him for about two weeks and finally he said, "All right. I'll have him in and buy one picture."

He had me in. I drew one picture, which I captioned "Quick Henry, the Flit!"—and it was published.

Then they hired me to do two more—and 17 years later I was still doing them.

The only good thing Adolf Hitler did in starting World II was that he enabled me to join the Army and finally stop drawing "Quick Henry, the Flit! "

I had drawn them by the millions—newspaper ads magazine ads, booklets, window displays, 24-sheet posters, even "Quick Henry, the Flit!" animated cartoons. Flit was pouring out of my ears and beginning to itch me.

Flit sales grew wildly. A song was written about it.the only other comparable campaign was the four-line Burma Shave highway signs.

Geisel simply sailed financially through the Depression years.

And, his contract allowed him considerable freedom—all he had to do was submit his Flit material on time—otherwise, he could do 'most anything else, except, of course, Fly-Tox material.

He could, and did, complete a year's worth of Flit! material in three months, leaving him the rest of the year free.

Readers of the Dr. Seuss books may wonder about the fantastical creatures and the even more fantastical locales Geisel drew. He remembered the animals at the Springfield Zoo—and how he had drawn them mis-shapen and, well, bizarre.

And the locales? He and Helen toured Greece during the spring of 1928 and toured elsewhere—for their first anniversary they traveled to La Jolla, a suburb of San Diego. Everything was fresh, new, clean, inviting, Flowers and plants in profusion everywhere. Views of the Pacific and California and Mexico. La Jolla had a Mediterranean /Spanish look. They were enchanted and vowed to return.

They later toured Peru.

In fact, Ted and Helen were world travelers After nine years of marriage they had visited 30 countries. *The Lorax* (1971), his *paean* to the environment, was conceived and developed during a visit to Kenya (with his second wife Audrey).

Oh! The Places You'll Go! ...

A collection of schoolroom gaffes was published in England under the title *Schoolboy Howlers*. The Viking Press bought the United States publication rights and re-titled the book *Boners*. Geisel was hired to illustrated it—and a sequel, *More Boners*, this time American schoolroom mistakes, sent in to The Viking Press by U.S. teachers. Both were published in 1931. The illustration work on these titles gave Geisel an epiphany:

> That was a big Depression year. And although by Depression standards I as adequately paid a flat fee for illustrating these best sellers, I was money-worried. The two books were booming and I was not.
>
> This is the point when I first began to realize that if I hoped to succeed in the book world, I'd have to write as well as draw.

He was encouraged by a review in the *American News:*

offhand ... we should have said this would be a flop. But the inimitable illustrations of the renowned Dr. Seuss of *Judge, Life* and Flit fame, are not unlikely to put this over. They are simply swell.

With that encouragement, he wrote and illustrated a children's ABC book, full of Seussian animals with seven-teen colors of blue and three colors of red. He took it to publishers Bobbs Merrill, Viking Press, Simon and Schuster and others ...

... where it was promptly rejected. He abandoned it.

But many others—many others—had seen his Flit illustrations/cartoons over the years.
Flit begat Esso.
The Esso gasoline people hired him, and later Schaeffer Bock Beer, Ford, Atlas Products, New Departure Bearings, NBC Radio and Holly Sugar all hired him. None ever asked that his Seussian drawings ever be changed. None ever carried the byline Seuss; they didn't need to.
Serendipity again played a major part in his life.

In the summer of 1936 the Geisels sailed for Europe aboard the M.S. Kungsholm. They visited the Alps; Geisel saw intrepid Alp animals clinging to sheer Alp mountain outcroppings. They traveled to

Germany and saw the chill of the coming Nazi tide. Geisel was then thirty-two years old and the storm clouds of European politics left him saddened.

They returned on the same ship—the Kungsholm.

And Geisel found himself caught in the drone of the engine.

Da-da-DA, Da-Da-*DUM*. Dum-De-Da. De-De-Da.

There was some slight variation, but the rhythm stayed in his head.

He was on the ship for eight days on the way back. Eight days of listening to the SAME engine rhythm.

The drone of the ship's engine became the driving energy of Dr. Seuss's career. It was as simple as that.

Da-da-Da, Da-Da-DUM. Dum-D*e-Da,* De-De-Pa. Geisel may not have known what he was hearing but the rhythm was hypnotic. Once captured by it, he was hooked. The rhythm didn't leave his head.

He didn't know what he was hearing, but there was a name for it. He might have heard the name at Dartmouth or Oxford; if he did, he probably forgot it.

He was hearing the rhythm of:

>'Twas the night before Christmas …
>
>… or …
>
>He flies through the air with the greatest of ease …

He was hearing *anapestic tetrameter* (or something close to it), which dates as far back as the ancient Greeks, who used it as a marching beat.

And so he had the rhythm; now he needed text to match. As he later recalled:

> I was on a long, stormy crossing of the Atlantic, and it was too rough to go out on deck. Everybody in the ship just sat in the bar for a week, listening to the engines turn over: da-da-ta-ta, da-da-ta-ta, da-da-ta-ta ...
>
> To keep from going nuts, I began reciting silly words to the rhythm of the engines. Out of nowhere, I found myself saying, "And that is a story no one can beat; and to think that I saw it on Mulberry Street."
>
> When I finally got off the ship, the refrain kept going through my head. I couldn't shake it. To therapeutize myself I added more words to it.

Mulberry Street was, of course, in his home town of Springfield.

Marrying text and rhythm and illustrations was not easy—what he perhaps knew instinctively, but did not or could not verbalize was: *the rhythm dictated the story and the rhythm galloped.*

Without knowing quite why, he may have sensed it was a perfect rhythm for a children's book.

And, as asides to the reader: all text begins on a right side page—page 1, as in this book. Pages 2 and 3 are facing or double pages, 4 and 5 are double pages, and so on. In regular textual material, there is a white "gutter" between pages. Geisel drew illustrations which were one picture for the facing or double pages—there was no separation between pages 2 and 3, 4 and 5, and on ... and, more importantly, again, probably instinctively, he added two important concepts:

- the action always move to the right, to keep readers turning the pages;
- characters and situations grew more and more fantastical, stranger and stranger, page after page until the action ended, as "the balloon broke" on the end page, leaving young readers to think, or say, *wow!* Or *whew!*

And to Think That I Saw It on Mulberry Street (1937);
McElligot's Pool (1947);
If I Ran the Zoo (1950) and
If I Ran the Circus (1956)

... all employ these techniques, as do many of the other Dr. Seuss books. When he did not use the anapestic tetrameter rhythm, his books were not quite as successful.

The rhythm gallops. Children can read it, sing it, SHOUT IT. They can dance to it.

As one young reader once said, "he has an imagination with a long tail." Geisel replied, "that kid will go far."

Additionally, on the copyright page, which is always "behind" the main title page, (on a left page) there is a set of numbers usually at, or toward, the bottom:

12345678

If the number 1 is on the list, the book is part of the first printing; when the printing is exhausted and the book goes back to press, the 1 is deleted and the line becomes:

2345678

Or sometimes backward:

98765432

There is no indication of how many copies were printed in the first (or subsequent) printings; some books have an average of 3,000 copies per printing.

Many—most of—the Dr. Seuss books have gone on and on and on: my copy of *McElligot's Pool* shows:

60 59 58 57

And my copy of *The Cat in the Hat* shows:

104 103 102 101 100 99

… which means there have been thousands and thousands, hundreds of thousands, of copies of these books printed and sold.

It took Geisel six months before he was pleased with his book. And here the story turns into legend. He took it to children's publishers in New York City, one two, three, turned it down, four, five, six. The rhyme scheme was too unusual; the drawings and characters far, far too unusual.

More and more: *No. No. No.*

Finally, at 27 rejections (although Dr. Seuss, with a twinkle in his eye, changed the number from time to time), he decided to give up.

He was on a New York sidewalk one day, with his manuscript under his arm, when he chanced to meet Marshall McClintock, who had been at Dartmouth one year behind Geisel.

The conversation went more or less, thus:

> "Ted, how are you? And what have you got?'
> "A book manuscript …"

Twenty-seven rejections …
Part of the text for his book was:
… *And this is a story no one can beat …*
… which became true.

McClintock had just been named editor at The Vanguard Press and they were standing outside its offices. McClintock invited Geisel into their offices, and he was introduced to James Henle, President of the Vanguard Press, and Evelyn Shrifte, staff editor.

Later that same day he had a contract.

Oh! The People You'll Meet! …

Geisel's life was full of *ifs*:

- If the wife of the McCann-Eriksson ad executive hadn't seen his *Judge* magazine work he wouldn't have had years of work for Flit;
- If Geisel had taken another ship to Europe and back he wouldn't have heard the anapestic tetrameter engine sounds which became his hallmark rhythm;
- If he had been five minutes earlier on the street or five minutes later he would have missed Marshall McClintock and missed his chance at The Vanguard Press.

Vanguard Press published *And To Think That I Saw It on Mulberry Street*. Reviews were exceptional:

> They say it's for children, but better get a copy for yourself and marvel at the good Dr. Seuss's improbable pictures and the moral tale of the little boy who exaggerated not wisely but too well. —*The New Yorker*

> Highly original and entertaining. Dr. Seuss' picture book partakes of the better qualities of those peculiarly American institutions, the funny papers and the tall tale. It is a masterly interpretation of the mind of a child in the art of creating one of those stories with which children often amuse themselves and bolster-up their self-respect.—*The New York Times*

The *Times* review hits on a key to Dr. Seuss' success; *there are never any adults shown in the Dr. Seuss books.*

> *They are all the secret worlds of children. Their imaginations at play.*

How is it that Geisel, as Dr. Seuss, could remain "true to the imagination of a small boy?" Helen Palmer Geisel, from the perspective of a loving spouse, later said, "his mind has never grown up."

Ted Geisel published two books with the Vanguard Press: *And To Think That I Saw It on Mulberry Street* (1937) and *The 500 Hats of Bartholomew Gubbins* (1938). For that book he put aside the anapestic tetrameter he had discovered and used regular text.

Then Bennett Cerf entered his life.

Cerf, a native New Yorker, graduated from Columbia University and initially wanted to be a stockbroker. That career was not for him—he quickly realized. He then joined the publishing firm of Boni and Liveright, run by Horace Liveright. Part of Boni and Liveright was the series The Modern Library. He was a speculator; the profits Liveright made from publishing he lost financing Broadway plays. He seemed to always need additional capital for Boni and Liveright. Cerf bought into the firm for $25,000; he eventually contributed another $25,000. to keep the publishing house in business. Two years later Cerf offered to buy The Modern Library. Liveright eventually sold it to Cerf for $200,000, plus an additional $15,000 "adviser fee" which he tacked on at the last moment.

Donald Klopfer joined Cerf, with an investment of $100,000. Two years after acquiring The Modern Library line, they had recovered all their investment, including Liveright's "adviser fee."

A *colophon* is a publishing house's signature icon. A symbol that is usually used on the lower spine of a hook, on the lower dust jacket for hardcover editions, sometimes on the main title page and in advertising and promotion.

Notable colophons are: the Viking ship for the Viking Press; a Bantam rooster for Bantam books; a penguin for Penguin Books; a Borzoi dog for Alfred Knopf (traditionally the most regal of all American firms); a castle for the Henry Regnery firm; a weather vane for the now-defunct firm, Paul Eriksson, Publisher (every which way the wind blows, a variation on *at random*); a kangaroo for Pocket Books; an owl for the Henry Holt firm and there are others.

In his memoir *At Random,* Cerf writes:

> Rockwell Kent had become a great friend of ours after he did the end papers for The Modern Library. I would say he was at that time the leading commercial artist in America. One day Rockwell dropped in at our office. He was sitting at my desk facing Donald, and we were talking about doing a few books on the side, when suddenly I got an inspiration and said, "I've got the name for our publishing house. We just said we were going to publish a few books on the side at random. Let's call it Random House."
>
> Donald liked it, and Rockwell Kent, said "That's a great name. I'll draw your trademark. So sitting at my desk he took out a piece of paper and in a few minutes drew Random House, which has been our colophon ever since."

Now with The Modern Library and their newly-minted colophon, which appeared in many variations over the years, Random House grew. Cerf brought in authors Eugene O'Neill and Robinson Jeffers, Msrcel Proust, Gertrude Stein, W. H. Auden, Stephen Spender, Havelock Ellis, George Bernard Shaw, William Saroyan, Budd Schulberg ... and others.

Cerf bought the financially-struggling firm of Smith and Haas, and got its authors, including William Faulkner, Andre Malraux, and Robert Graves.

And then Cerf entered Ted Geisel's life. At the urging of Cerf s wife Phyllis, he began a children's book line; the author he most wanted was Geisel. But Geisel was legally obligated to The Vanguard Press, so Cerf did the easiest thing; Random House bought the Vanguard Press to bring Geisel to Random House.

Cerf didn't know what Geisel wanted to publish next and perhaps didn't care. Geisel's next project was not a success but now first editions are highly prized by Seuss collectors.

It was *The Seven Lady Godivas*; a retelling of the Lady Godiva fable, with not one but seven naked Godivas. But Geisel's naked ladies were as lumpy and mal-formed as all the other Seuss creatures—in short, naked, but not one iota erotic. Adults weren't interested and librarians didn't want naked ladies *in any form,* in the *kiddie lit* shelves of their libraries.

Although it was the lowest point in Geisel's career, neither Cerf nor Geisel were discouraged.

Random House would be Geisel's publishing home for the rest of his career and bringing Geisel to Random House was

TIMESLESS (PEN) NAMES

eventually a huge coup for Cerf professionally and financially. Bennett Cerf's gamble on Dr. Seuss would pay off, quite literally for decades.

Another aside for readers: books which stay in print for more that one year are called "backlist" books; when they are first published, they appear in the front of publisher's catalogs, traditionally issued twice a year. As new seasons and new titles appear, they are slowly pushed toward the *back* of the catalogs. Books that stays in print for more than one year are eventual goldmines for publishers as all the expenses associated with editing and printing the book are factored into the first year's sales.

Sales and profits from backlist books help pay for new titles. Publishers can't survive on books that only have limited, one-year sales.

Think of classic authors: Hemingway, Faulkner—John Steinbeck. Steinbeck's *The Grapes of Wrath* was first published by The Viking Press in 1939 and still sells in the millions of dollars each year, estimated six to ten million in sales per year. Now. With very little effort by The Viking Press, except making sure there are copies in the warehouse to ship out and occasionally changing the hardcover dust jacket.

The second book for Cerf and Random House was *The King's Stilts*, and it also was in prose, not in rhyme. While *The Seven Lady Godivas* was Ted Geisel's nadir, in sales, *The King's Stilts* was a close second. It sold 4,648 copies during the first year of publication, but only 394 copies the second year. Bennett Cerf must have thought to himself, *Random House bought the Vanguard Press to bring Ted Geisel to our new children's lit.*

department, but his first two titles have been disasters ... was this all a huge mistake? But he was the very soul of tact to Geisel—waiting and hoping for better ...

Geisel was taking a break from work one day when a slight breeze from an open window blew a drawing of an elephant across a drawing of a tree.

> *What would an elephant be doing in a tree?* he thought.
> *Hatching an egg,* of course.

That led to feverish but long-term work.

And To Think That I Saw In on Mulberry Street taught children that their imaginations were as real as Marco's—the little hero, and occasionally they should—or must—shield their imaginations from adults.

And so Dr. Seuss eventually finished *Horton Hatches the Egg*. It was in his galloping anapestic tetrameter; it had a hero, Horton, which children could identify with and he had made a promise *("He meant what he said and he said what he meant ...")* but had trouble keeping it. It was in the first-person "I" form and children could chant it: *I said what I meant and I meant what I said ...* and they well understood: *if you make a promise you must keep it.*

The New York Times reviewed it thus:

> A moral is a new thing to find in a Dr. Seuss book, but it doesn't interfere with the hilarity with which he juggles an elephant up a tree. To an adult the tale seems a little less inevitable in its nonsense,

but neither young nor old are going to quibble with the fantastic comedy of his pictures.

Bennett Cerf and editors at Random House loved it. And when Geisel asked for a royalty advance of $500 to help buy a home in La Jolla, Cerf immediately sent it. Ted and Helen moved to La Jolla—and the purchase price of their home was—in 1940 dollars—$8,000. (Imagine: what would a La Jolla home with a view of the Pacific would bring today?)

The La Jolla purchase was his permanent home; he seldom left it—and why should he?

Then the coming war interrupted Dr. Seuss.

A drawing he had done was passed along by a friend to Ralph Ingersoll, who had left the staff of *The New Yorker*, to start a very liberal newspaper, *PM*, for New York City. The very idea amused Dr. Seuss: *PM took no advertising*, which made it a sister to *Judge*, which *got no advertising*.

Dr. Seuss contributed editorial illustrations or cartoons; he called Charles Lindbergh "one of our nation's most irritating heros," and was a very early critic of Hitler.

His cartoons was acidic—very acidic: Australia was shown as a kangaroo with its tail being eaten by the Japanese and Nazis were depicted as dachshunds, at least until American dachshund owners protested.

His World War Two cartoons for *PM* have been published in book form, cited in the Bibliography.

(And what of *PM*, Ingersoll's experiment in ultra-liberal, advertising-free journalism? It lasted from June 1940 to June 1948, but during its tenure, besides Geisel, contributors included: Haywood Hale Broun; Dorothy Parker; Ernest Hemingway; James Thurber; Malcolm Cowley; Tip O'Neill [Later Speaker of the U.S House of Representatives] and Ben Hecht. Liberals all.)

Before leaving New York, Geisel was inducted into the U.S. Army as a Captain and assigned to the Information and Entertainment Division, in Hollywood.

There, he joined director Frank Capra *(It Happened One Night; Mr. Smith Goes to Washington; It's a Wonderful Life)*, composer Meredith Willson *(The Music Man)*, novelist Irving Wallace, animators Chuck Jones *(Bugs Bunny)*, Friz Freleng and a gaggle of others.

Geisel worked on a team to produce training films:

> ... to teach G.I.s cleanliness, avoidance of VD and other military matters. Geisel and company learned if they showed average spokesmen in the films, recruits wouldn't listen; if they used Hollywood actors, the G.I.s jeered at the screen. They *would* pay attention to cartoons, so Geisel and his crew created Private Snafu to explain things.
>
> Snafu was, was, of course, Army slang for Situation Normal All *F*-ked *Up*. They changed SNAFU to Situation Normal All *Fouled* Up. The G.I.s still loved it.

When World War Two ended and Geisel was free from the distractions of Private Snafu and such, he retuned to his Dr. Seuss books. It became a near-annual event when he traveled from La Jolla to New York to hand-deliver a Seuss manuscript to the New York offices of Random House. And, like others whose experiences shaped their craft, he simply got better and better. His most critical and financial successes came after World War Two.

His post-war books were:

1947: *McElligot's Pool*
1948: *Thidwick the Big-Hearted Moose*
1949: *Barththolomew and the Oobleck*
1950: *If I Ran the Zoo*
1953: *Scrambled Eggs Super!*
1954: *Horton Hears a Who!*

In 1954, Geisel learned that his alma mater, Dartmouth, planned to grant him an honorary degree.

But the same year his wife Helen felt pain in her feet and ankles. Two days later she checked into the Scripps Metabolic Clinic; she had numbness in her arms, hands, and face and she could not swallow. She had Guillian-Barre Syndrome and was placed in an iron lung. She was unable to sit up without help.

Throughout his life, Ted Geisel had coasted along; he had a successful career and lived on a mountaintop. Except for his sister's death in Springfield, tragedy had never struck him. But this was *serious*.

Helen was moved to a rehabilitation center for extensive treatment. Geisel was left alone—everything she had done he now had to do alone—he had never balanced his checkbook or even made a pot of coffee.

A year after he heard about his Dartmouth honor, he bought an academic gown at a San Diego second-hand store, trekked to Dartmouth and received his honorary degree, (along with Robert Frost) thus making Dr. Seuss legitimate. It should be: Dr. Dr. Seuss, he said. Helen was, by then, well enough to travel with him to Dartmouth.

He then began *If I Ran the Circus*, patterned after *If I Ran the Zoo*.

He had been asked by William Spaulding, publisher of the firm Houghton Mifflin to write a children's book with no more than 225 words—but there was a problem—Geisel was legally bound to Random House. Spaulding would somehow have to work with Bennett Cerf and Random House to get Geisel. The resolution was ingenious; Geisel's book would be split fifty-fifty: Houghton Mifflin could have educational rights—legal rights to sell copies to schools and such and Random House would have "trade rights," rights to sell the book in bookstores and other non-educational outlets. To the "book trade," as it was, and still is, called.

With *If I Ran the Circus* completed, Geisel began the new book. It was very nearly impossible. Houghton Mifflin wanted a book better than any children's book ever published.

Impossible for Dr. Seuss and impossible even for Ted Geisel.

It took him a full year. He examined every word, every possible combination of the 225 words in the word list. He thought he had a combination with Queen and Zebra, but discovered they weren't on the list.

He finally found what he was looking for:

I read (the list) forty times and got more and more discouraged. It was like trying to make strudel without the strudel. I was desperate so I decided to read it once more. The first words that rhymed would be the title of my book and I'd go from there. I found "cat" and then I found "hat." That's genius you see!

Genius indeed. But wasn't it Thomas Edison, who once said, genius is "one percent inspiration and 99 percent perspiration"?

Geisel slaved at that book—which changed children's literature forever. He worked and he thought and he thought and he worked—the Cat began to take over the story—a Cat wearing a red and white striped top hat. And a bow tie—tied with three loops, not two. And white gloves like early Mickey Mouse cartoons.

It didn't quite have his usual anapestic tetrameter, but the rhyme carried the story. In some of the Seuss books, the story begins with a daydream—*And To Think That I Saw It on Mulberry Street*, as an example—but in this book, the Cat simply appears.

The Cat is a trickster figure, a technique as old as storytelling itself, as in the Kokopelli trickster figure of the American Indian southwest. The Cat is magical and does not think logically—it appeals to the rebellious nature of all children.

But the Cat's wild nature is balanced by the two children—who are worried about what will happen and what their parents will say. Indeed, it's every child's nightmare that their house will somehow be demolished and their Mother will appear at the front door at just the wrong moment.

The Cat does demolish the house—pandemonium everywhere. Everything a mess. The children look on helplessly. The Cat brings out two creatures Thing I and Thing 2; the Cat assures the children that they are harmless, but they make things even worse. Finally the Cat brings out a cleaning machine to straighten everything out.

The Cat in the Hat was an instant success. It was everything standard *kiddie lit* books were not: it was written from the child's point of view; every child could read it; it encouraged mayhem and making a mess of everything and it had no real moral lesson.

Perfect!

And children could read it by themselves—without adult supervision.

Random House bookstore sales skyrocketed and quickly outsold the Houghton Mifflin educational market.

> Within three years the book had sold nearly a million copies and had editions in French, Chinese, Swedish and Braille.

Reviews poured in: *The New York Times, The New York Herald Tribune, The Chicago Sunday Tribune,* and *The Saturday Review of Literature*—all enthusiastic.

And then—it became the only book that established a whole publishing program. The next time Geisel traveled to New York and the Random House offices, Phyllis Cerf, Bennett Cerf s wife took him to lunch. She proposed that *The Cat in the Hat* should continue to be published in a large format—roughly 8½ by 11 inches in hardcover, but that a whole new series should be published in mini-formats for pre-schoolers and even earlier.

Thus the Cat—*The Cat in the Hat*—by itself begat Beginner Books, which became a separate room inside the Random House house, if you will. And very few cats can claim they established a publishing program by themselves.

Ted—and Helen Geisel—were both intrigued. They invested in Beginner Books, as did Phyllis Cerf, Bennett Cerf's wife.

And indeed, some child experts have suggested pre-beginner books—that babies be read to *while in the womb*—Geisel, presumably, would agree.

But before Geisel could begin Beginner Books he had to complete another title he promised to Random House.

Christmas.

Something about Christmas.

And for the first time he featured an adult. A bad guy, as kids might say.

The Grinch.

He portrayed the Grinch with a remarkably apt description, which children—especially children—could understand: he hated Christmas "because his heart was two sizes too small."

And with that beginning Geisel created a fable just as endearing and timeless as "Twas the Night Before Christmas." Geisel said the Grinch had hated Christmas for 53 years—Geisel was 53 years old when he wrote it.

The Grinch steals all the presents from the Whos in Whoville—appearing again—but Christmas went on anyway: it isn't presents but love that makes Christmas.

But Geisel had a problem—*he didn't know how to end the book.*

He *never* knew how to end the book:

> I got hung up getting the Grinch out of the mess. I got into a situation where I sounded like a second-fate preacher or some biblical truism. Finally in desperation ... without making any statement wherever, I showed the Grinch and the Whos together at the table, and making a pun of the Grinch carving the "roast beast" ... I had gone through thousands of religious choices, and then after three months it came out like that.

And the hard *GR* sound of Grinch is just perfect for a "bad guy."

Like Lewis Carroll with *chortle,* Geisel added a new definition to the language:

> Grinch: any sour, pessimistic person who dismisses love and attempts to deprive others of happiness.

His moral in *The Grinch* ...

> Maybe Christmas doesn't come from a store.
> Maybe Christmas ... means a little bit more!

And while *The Cat in the Hat* was setting sales records, the first printing of *The Grinch* ... was 50,000 copies.

Critics again raved about a new Dr. Seuss books: *The Saturday Review of Literature; The San Francisco Chronicle, The New York Times; The New York Herald Tribune* and *Kirkus*, the book review service, among others, were all overwhelmingly enthusiastic.

Thereafter, Geisel published *The Cat in the Hat Comes Back*, which was *good* Dr. Seuss but not *great* Dr. Seuss.

In 1957, Helen Geisel was taken to the nearby Scripps Clinic diagnosed with dizziness and confusion. The diagnosis: she had suffered a small stroke.

Geisel had covered Christmas with *The Grinch* ... he subsequently tackled another holiday/celebration which virtually guaranteed sales to, and for, children: *Happy Birthday to You! was* published in 1959.

Bennett Cerf had a thought—and made a bet—could Dr. Seuss write a book with only 50 words? Geisel had access to 225 words for *The Cat in the Hat*. Could he be as successful with just 50? The bet was for $50.

Geisel's eventual title: *Green Eggs and Ham,* an obvious play on *ham and eggs.*

Chuck Jones, of Bugs Bunny fame, clearly saw what Geisel was doing: he was using the reversal of a common phrase, but using it like the Pennsylvania Dutch, who are not Dutch at all but German. (Pennsylvania Dutch is a corruption of *Deutsch,* the German word for German); and he was using the phrase like the Yiddish language, which employed phrases like "throw Mother from the train, a kiss."

That Sam-I-am!

Much later Geisel said it was the only Dr. Seuss hook "that still makes me laugh."

And Ted Geisel won the $50 bet with Bennett Cerf.

The Cat in the Hat, *The Grinch* ... *Green Eggs and Ham*—all critical and financial successes for Dr. Seuss.

The price of fame: after *Green Eggs and Ham* was published and when Boy Scouts, Cub Scouts, Girl Scouts, Brownie Scouts, various kids clubs, groups and such, all knew his La Jolla address, on his birthday, crew after crew came to his front door with platters of green eggs and ham.

"Vile stuff," he said.

One birthday, to get away, Ted and Helen and another couple decamped to Las Vegas. "They'll (the kids) never find me here," he said. The four had front-row seats to a splashy Las Vegas show. The first act was 20 nearly-buck naked women roaring onto the stage on 20 motorcycles.

"I can't tell what kind of motorcycles they are," Geisel said.

"I think you're missing something," his friend said.

In late 1961, the Geisels got a call from Donald Klopfer, at Random House. The Geisels had invested in Beginner Books; Klopfer told them that Grolier, another publisher, wanted to begin a children's book club and wanted Dr. Seuss books, among others.

The Geisels refused; Grolier could have Dr. Seuss titles but no others—none from any other publisher. Klopfer was astonished, but the Geisels still refused. Grolier could distribute Dr. Seuss titles *and* other Beginner Books titles, but none from any other publisher. Eventually Grolier agreed. Forty years later, Grolier had paid more than forty million dollars to Beginner Books, and, in the process, had become the nation's largest children's book club.

Geisel had created another pseudonym: Theo LeSieg, *Geisel* backward, and with that, he added a new line of books: he would write the text and others would contribute the illustrations. *Ten Apples Up on Top* came first, then *I Wish I Had Duck Feet* and *Come Over to My House*—and others—they were not quite top-of-the-line Seuss, but they did fit Beginner Books and they did sell.

In 1996, Geisel checked: his stock in Beginner Books had made him not just a millionaire, but a multi-millionaire.

Cathy Goldsmith, president and publisher of Random House's Beginning Books line recently said, "We sell more Dr. Seuss books today then we did when he was alive. The books stand the test of times."

To date, Random House has sold more than 16 million copies of *The Cat in the Hat* in multiple editions; annual sales average 500,000 copies. The book has been translated into Spanish, French, German, Dutch, Italian, Portuguese, Latin, Chinese, Japanese, Icelandic, Norwegian, Russian, Polish, Yiddish, Hebrew, Estonian, Serbian and Greek.

Random House staged a "60 (and a Half)" celebration of the publication of *The Cat …* in September, 2017.

"We know Ted would be overjoyed by *The Cat in the Hat*'s enduring legacy, and tickled by this whimsical celebration of a book that he wrote to inspire children to love to read. *The Cat in the Hat*'s impact has been extraordinary and we only wish Ted could be here to see it today."

Of the Seuss stories she said, "There's always something unexpected; they're not formulaic. You remember them quite vividly. It's hard to get bored with Seuss. He's entertaining for the adult as well as the child."

Geisel had Dr. Seuss books, Beginner Books and now Theo LeSieg—and then Chuck Jones re-entered the picture. Jones, from Geisel's Private Snafu Army period ...

> ... believed that Dr. Seuss material could, and should, be made into a cartoon special for television. Typical negotiations followed, via Geisel's agents, potential sponsors, the Geisels and assorted friends and others.
>
> It was early in 1966 and the calendar made the choice: by the end of the year, Jones could have *The Grinch* ready for holiday viewing.
>
> Jones moved *The Grinch* in animation without using any of the slapdash techniques of the time. Typical cartoons then used abbreviated action—backgrounds repeated (the same trees would reappear behind running figures), for instance and voices didn't quite match actions. Jones used full-action techniques: 25,000 drawings instead of a typical cartoon with 2,000 drawings.
>
> The Grinch had to be reinvented. Colors—which colors should be used? What kind of a voice? How would the Whos be animated? And the length?—typically the Grinch story could be read aloud to an audience in less than 15 minutes. It had to be lengthened to almost a half hour (minus time for

commercials). Would the plot have to be changed or added to?

Geisel wanted the Grinch to be black-and-white—but Jones suggested his eyes be a jealous green.

And eventually narrating the story was—the man with the perfect Grinch-y voice—Boris Karloff. CBS-TV bought The Grinch, paying MGM $315,000 for two annual showings in 1966 and 1967. Chuck Jones predicted it would be rerun "for the next ten years."

He was wrong—*How the Grinch Stole Christinas!* has become an annual holiday event along with Dickens' *A Christmas Carol* and another cartoon classic, *Charlie Brown's Christmas* by Charles Schultz. Some things should go on forever. *How the Grinch Stole Christmas!* is one—a holiday story with an obvious holiday moral, without being preachy or being overly religious. In other words, perfect for everyone.

And then … and then … On the morning of October 23, 1967, the housekeeper entered the Geisel's home and found no one up. That in itself was not unusual. Ted and Helen had separate bedrooms and he often slept late. The housekeep, Alberta Shaw, entered Helen's room …

… and found her dead. Sometime during the night, she had taken her own life, over-dosing with sodium pentobarbital tablets.

No one knows much pain she may have been in; she had left a note for Ted, believing herself a failure.

Her death was published in the local newspapers and quickly sent across the country by the wire services.

As he had done with the death of his sister decades before, in Springfield, Massachusetts, Geisel maintained a stoic silence. Always. Parts of the Geisel fortune went to the La Jolla Museum's Art-Reference Library, which was renamed in her honor. Her share of the Geisel royalties were to Dartmouth and other royalties and income went into the nonprofit Seuss Foundation. It was considerable.

Ted and Helen Geisel had known Audrey Dimond, a La Jolla friend.

In June, 1968, he and she traveled to Reno, where they spent the requisite period of waiting time and were married.

And in September, 1970, they traveled to Kenya. One afternoon, at the Mount Kenya Safari Club, he witnessed a herd of elephants passing on the horizon. He was galvanized into action. The result was *The Lorax*, (1971) his *paean* to the environment. It became his most controversial book.

His readers would never have known that, by the 1970s, his health was slowly fading. One morning in 1975, he couldn't see. He called Audrey in a panic. She feared cataracts; the diagnosis was cataracts *and* glaucoma. He enduring five years of operations—which contributed to his 1978 book, *I Can See with My Eyes Shutl*

Old age crept closer.

During a dental exam, a lesion was discovered at the base of his tongue—it was cancerous and potentially very dangerous.

An operation placed an implant under his tongue to neutralize the cancer.

In 1985, he won the Pulitzer Prize.

"It was," he said, "usually given to adults. I'm a writer who has to eat with the children before the adults eat." And, that same year, Audrey tricked him into going to Princeton University where he received an honorary degree. When he got up to receive his diploma, the entire graduating class rose and chanted the entire text of *Green Eggs and Ham*.

He considered the health problems he had suffered through. The eye problems, the mouth cancer—and decided to write a book for adults. Those in the same lifespan as he; those with health problems or those who anticipated health problems. He had often said "adults are only obsolete children—and to hell with 'em."

But this book was for them. The title: *You're Only Old Once!* (Dr. Seuss loved using exclamation points in his titles). He recalled then—as now—the costs of modern medicine.

Staff people at Random House were worried that adults wouldn't buy a Dr. Seuss book. Even the first and second generation of Dr. Seuss youngsters had probably forgotten about him long ago—they were, after all, grandparents themselves by now.

But Ted Geisel *and* Dr. Seuss knew—they knew young readers hadn't forgotten, as they grew older themselves. And he was right when Random House staff members—far younger than he—were decidedly wrong. The first printing was 200,000 copies. It hit the number one spot on *The New York Times* best seller lists and by the end of six months had sold 600,000 copies.

His mouth cancer problem had resulted in an infection of his jaw, impossible to eradicate. He became increasingly infirm with bouts of gout and loss of hearing and often turned down invitations outside La Jolla.

He then remembered the callow—the cynical—motto from his college years: "Oh! The Places You'll Go. The People You'll Meet."

His next book, *Oh! The Places You'll Go!* also hit *The New York Times* best seller lists and stayed there for more than two years. It sold, during that time, 1,500,000 copies. It was the last book published during his lifetime.

In 1991, critic Clifton Fadiman wrote, with sales of *only* 200 million, Seuss "has become part of the environment, a kind of public utility. Nothing in the history of books for children comes within hailing distance of this phenomenon."

Now, estimates are 600 million Dr. Seuss books have been sold.

Slowly, Ted Geisel put his work away. There was no pain, no real suffering. He began sleeping on a couch in his studio. He awoke once and asked his wife, "am I dead yet?"

Theodor Geisel died quietly September 24, 1991, at 87.

But his legacy continued—there were Dr. Seuss books published posthumously; and the earlier ones were reprinted and reprinted.

Dr. Seuss had reached the highest pantheon of literature—along with Lewis Carroll, Mark Twain and George Orwell.

Their books will live forever.

Notes

Page

1 "… who was born in Daresbury …" Wood, *The Snark Was a Boojum*, pp. 3–4.

5 "The Mystery of Lewis Carroll" retrieved from the website publicdomainreview.org

21 "the first truly American writer …" William Faulkner in *Faulkner at Nagano*, p. 88.

21 "All modern literature comes from one book …" Ernest Hemingway in *Green Hills of Africa*, p. 22.

23 "It was as Samuel Clemens …" Bernard Taper in *Mark Twain's San Francisco*, p. xi.

24 "Parody, burlesque …" Ibid. p. xi.

25 "I am tearing along …" Justin Kaplan, *Mr. Clemens and Mark Twain*, p. 197.

27 "Although commentators differ …" Shelly Fisher Fishkin, *Was Huck Black?* p. 3.

27 "Mark Twain helped …" Fishkin, p. 5.

43 "In many respects, Orwell himself did not have …" Thomas E. Ricks, *Churchill and Orwell: The Fight for Freedom*, p.126.

43 "During the war …" Louis Menard, "Honest, Decent, Wrong: The invention of George Orwell," *The New Yorker*, Jan. 27, 2003.

44 "I saw a little boy …" Orwell, Preface to the Ukrainian edition of *Animal Farm*.

45	"I believe *Gulliver's Travels* …" W. J. West, *The Larger Evils*, p. 62.
45	"Seven Commandments …" *Animal Farm*, U.S. ed. p. 21.
47	"It was a bright cold day in April …" Orwell, *1984*, U.S. ed., p. 3.
52	"Jura is mountainous …" Wikipedia entry: Jura.
52	"His family owned an estate …" McCrum, "The masterpiece that killed Orwell," *The Guardian*, July 8, 2015.
53	"In May, 1946 …" Ibid.
54	"It was a desperate …" Ibid.,
54	"When he was alive …" Ricks, p. 246.
55	"In the post 9/11 era …" Ibid., 255.
55	"It is a warfare …" Orwell, in Ricks, p. 255.
56	"It was a bright cold day in April …" Orwell, *1984*, U.S. ed., p. 3.
56	"The Ministry of Truth …"Orwell, U.S. ed., p. 5.
58	"He was …" *Time* magazine wrote …," Fensch, *The Man Who Was Dr. Seuss*," p. 178.
60	"… took a pencil …" Ibid., p. 29.
60	"Our model that day …, " Geisel, in Fensch, p. 30.
61	"Geisel was doing …" Fensch, *The Man Who Was* … p. 30–31.
62	"He never had any money …" Ibid. p. 38.
62	"He was not gregarious …" Ibid., p. 40.
64	"English and writing …" Ibid. , p. 42.
64	"With the imagery of …" Ibid., p.44.
65	"Any woman who could …" Ibid., 44.
65	"i have tramped …" Geisel in Fensch, *The Man Who* …, p. 49.

66	"I'd been working for *Judge* ..." Geisel in Fensch, p. 53–54.
69	"That was a big Depression year ..." Ibid., p. 57.
69	"offhand, we should have said ..." Ibid., p. 57–58.
70	"In the summer of 1936 ..." Ibid., p. 63.
71	"I was on a long, stormy ..." Ibid., p. 64.
76	*The New Yorker* and *The New York Times* reviews in Fensch, p. 69–70.
78	"Rockwell Kent ..." In Bennett Cerf, *At Random,* (New York: Random House, 1977) in Fensch, p. 74.
81	"A moral is a new thing ..." Ibid. p. 84.
82	History of *PM*, Wikipedia entry.
83	"...to teach G.I.s cleanliness ..." in Fensch, p. 67.
83	"I read (the list) forty times ..." Geisel, in Fensch, p. 118.
87	"Within three years ..." Morgan and Morgan, *Dr Seuss and Mr. Geisel,* in Fensch, p. 123.
88	"His heart was two sizes too small" is the now-famous description of The Grinch, by Geisel
89	"I got hung up getting the Grinch ..." Morgan and Morgan in Fensch, p. 127.
92	"Cathy Goldsmith ..." "'The Cat in the Hat' at 60 (and a Half)", by Emma Kantor, *Publishers Weekly,* September 7, 2017.
93	"... believed that Dr. Seuss material could, and should," in Fensch, pp. 52–53,
97	"He has become part of the environment..."Clifton Fadiman, Introduction, *Six by Seuss* (New York: Random House, 1991), p. 6.
97	"600 million ..." Wikipedia entry Dr. Seuss.

Bibliography

Bower, Gordon. *Inside George Orwell: A Biography.* New York: Palgrave Macmillan, 2003.

Burgess, Anthony. *1986.* London: Hutchison, 1978.

Carroll, Lewis. *Alice in Wonderland.* 1865.

____. *Through the Looking-Glass and What Alice Found There.* 1871.

Cohen, Morton. *Lewis Carroll: A Biography.* New York: Vintage Books, 1996.

Crick, George. *George Orwell: A Life.* Boston: Atlantic-Little Brown, 1980.

Dean, Michelle. "The Search for Facts in a Post-Fact World." *Wired* magazine, Oct., 2017.

Fensch, Thomas. *Alice in Acidland.* Cranbury, N. J.: A.S. Barnes Co., 1970.

____. *The Man Who Was Dr. Seuss: The Life and Work of Theodor Geisel.* N. Chesterfield, Va.: New Century Books, 2000.

____. *Of Sneetches and Whos and the Good Dr. Seuss: Essays on the Writings and Life of Theodor Geisel.* N. Chesterfield, Va., New Century Books, 1997, 2015.

Fishkin, Shelly Fisher. *Was Huck Black? Mark Twain and African-American Voices.* New York and Oxford: Oxford University Press, 1993.

Gardner, Martin. *The Annotated Alice.* New York: W.W. Norton, 2015.

Geisel, Theodor "Dr. Seuss." *And To Think That I Saw It on Mulberry Street.* New York: The Vanguard Press, 1937.

____. *Cat in the Hat, The.* New York: Random House, 1957.

____. *Green Eggs and Ham.* New York: Random House, 1960.

____. *How the Grinch Stole Christmas!* New York: Random House, 1957.

Griset, Rich. "Somebody's Watching You: If everything we do is tracked or caught on camera what next?" *Chesterfield* (Va.) *Monthly,* Nov. 2014.

Hinde, Thomas, Intro. *Lewis Carroll: Looking-Glass Letters.* London: Collins & Brown, 1991.

Hitchens, Christopher. *Why Orwell Matters.* New York: Basic Books, 2003.

Hoffman, Andrew. *Inventing Mark Twain: The Lives of Samuel Langhorne Clemens.* New York: Wm. Morrow, 1997.

Howe, Irving. *Orwell's Nineteen Eighty-Four: Text, Sources, Criticism.* New York: Harcourt Brace and World, 1963.

Hudson, Derek. *Lewis Carroll.* London: Constable, 1954.

Humorous Verse of Lewis Carroll, The. New York: Dover Publications, 1960.

Kantor, Emma. "'The Cat in the Hat' at 60 (and a Half)," *Publishers Weekly*, September 7, 2017.

Kaplan, Justin. Mr. *Clemens and Mark Twain*. New York: Simon and Schuster, 1983.

Lauber, John. *The Making of Mark Twain*. New York: Farrar, Strauss 8e Giroux, 1985.

Lennon, Florence Becker. *Victoria Through the Looking-Glass: The Life of Lewis Carroll*. New York: Simon and Schuster, 1945.

Lewis, Peter. *George Orwell: The Road to 1984*. New York: Harcourt Brace Jovanovich, 1981.

McCrum, Robert. "The masterpiece that killed George Orwell." *The Guardian*, July, 8, 2015.

Menard, Louis. "Honest, Decent, Wrong: The invention of George Orwell." *The New Yorker*, Jan. 27, 2003.

Meyers, Jeffrey. *Orwell: Wintery Conscience of a Generation*. New York: W.W. Norton, 2000.

Minear, Richard H. *Dr. Seuss Goes to War: The World War Two Editorial Cartoon of Theodor Seuss Geisel*. New York: The New Press, 1999.

Morgan, Judith and Neil Morgan. *Dr. Seuss and Mr. Geisel: A Biography*. New York: Random House, 1995.

Morris, Roy, Jr. *Lighting Out for the Territory: How Samuel Clemens Headed West and Became Mark Twain*. New York: Simon and Schuster, 2010.

Orwell, George. *Animal Farm*. London: Seeker and Warburg, 1945.

———. *1984*. London: Decker & Warburg, 1949.

Phillips, Robert. *Aspects of Alice: Lewis Carroll's Dreamchild as Seen Through the Critics' Looking-Glass, 1865-1971*. New York: The Vanguard Press, 1971.

Power, Ron. *Dangerous Water: A Biography of the Boy Who Became Mark Twain*. New York: Basic Books, 1999.

Ricks, Thomas E. *Churchill and Orwell: The Fight for Freedom*. New York: Penguin Books, 2017.

Rodden, John. *Scenes from an Afterlife: The Legacy of George Orwell* Wilmington, Del.: ISI Books, 2003.

Shelden, Michael. *Orwell: The Authorized Biography.* London: William Heinemann, 1991.

Steinbrink, Jeffrey. *Getting to be Mark Twain*. Berkeley: University of California Press, 1991.

Steinhoff, William. *George Orwell and the Origins of* 1984. Ann Arbor: The University of Michigan Press, 1975.

Taper, Bernard. *Mark Twain's San Francisco.* New York: McGraw-Hill, 1963.

Teacher, Lawrence, ed, *The Unabridged Mark Twain*. Philadelphia: The Running Press, 1976.

West, W. J. *The Larger Evils: Nineteen Eighty-Four—The Truth Behind the Satire*. Edinburgh, Eng.: Canongate Press, 1992.

Wood, James Playsted. *The Snark Was a Boojum: A Life of Lewis Carroll*. New York: Pantheon Books, 1966.

Introduction Redux

- Mark Twain and Dr. Seuss were from the United States, Lewis Carroll and George Orwell were from England;
- Lewis Carroll was unmarried, Dr. Seuss married but childless, George Orwell adopted a child, only Mark Twain had a regular family;
- Lewis Carroll and Dr. Seuss specialized in children's literature, Mark Twain and George Orwell specialized in adult literature;
- All traveled outside their home country;
- Orwell died early, rushing to finish his masterwork, *1984*, while seriously ill;
- All spent years perfecting their craft;
- All developed their pen names in unique ways;
- Lewis Carroll often refused to acknowledge his pen name—while Orwell used his pen name to hide his personal background. Mark Twain and Dr. Seuss largely embraced their pseudonyms.

About the author ...

THOMAS FENSCH has published non-fiction books since 1970; a partial list is at the front of this book.

He has published five books on John Steinbeck, two on Theodor "Dr. Seuss" Geisel, two on James Thurber, one each on Oskar Schindler, Hemingway and John Howard Griffin, the author of *Black Like Me*, and other non-fiction titles.

Fensch has a doctorate from Syracuse University and lives outside Richmond, Va.

www.ingramcontent.com/pod-product-compliance
Lightning Source LLC
Chambersburg PA
CBHW070928160426
43193CB00011B/1606